Elizabeth Taylor and Richard Burton: A Ron Hollywood

By Charles River Editors

Burton and Taylor in *Cleopatra*

About Charles River Editors

Charles River Editors was founded by Harvard and MIT alumni to provide superior editing and original writing services, with the expertise to create digital content for publishers across a vast range of subject matter. In addition to providing original digital content for third party publishers, Charles River Editors republishes civilization's greatest literary works, bringing them to a new generation via ebooks.

Sign up here to receive updates about free books as we publish them, and visit Our Kindle Author Page to browse today's free promotions and our most recently published Kindle titles.

Introduction

Burton and Julie Andrews in *Camelot*

Richard Burton (1925-1984)

"You may be as vicious about me as you please. You will only do me justice." – Richard Burton

In the 1960s, the most popular actor in the world was Richard Burton, a hard-drinking Welshman who was nevertheless so professional that he was one of the preeminent stage performers of his day. In fact, he performed Shakespeare so magnificently that he was compared to British legend Laurence Olivier, and that success ultimately led to a film career that earned him 7 Academy Award nominations, as well as BAFTA and Golden Globe awards for Best Actor.

Given his accomplishments on the stage and in Hollywood, Burton became one of the world's most recognizable leading men, so it seemed fitting that he engaged in one of Hollywood's most legendary romances with Elizabeth Taylor while on the set of *Cleopatra*, one of the era's most notorious movies. In fact, his tumultuous relationship with Taylor, which included two marriages, dominated tabloids and remains the one thing most people associate with Burton today, despite the rest of his accomplishments.

Burton's high-profile marriage to Taylor helped bring attention, but it also led to more self-destructive behavior, and in a sense it represented the peak of Burton's career. Over the last decade of his life, Burton began appearing in mediocre films, and due to his declining health and constant drunkenness, his performances were mediocre as well, often involving incoherent slurring. The fast life ultimately caught up with him in 1984, when a cerebral hemorrhage killed him at the age of 58. Fittingly, it was the same cause of death that befell his alcoholic father in 1957, just as Burton was at the precipice of Hollywood stardom.

This book examines the life and career of one of Hollywood's biggest stars of the 1960s. Along with pictures of important people, places, and events, you will learn about Richard Burton like never before.

Elizabeth Taylor (1932-2011)

"I've always admitted that I'm ruled by my passions." – Elizabeth Taylor

Hollywood is full of cautionary tales for child actors like Judy Garland, Jackie Coogan, and Macaulay Culkin, who all soared to fame in their youth only to suffer family feuds, drug addiction, or other ill effects of becoming famous so early in life. Even those child actors for whom stardom was not traumatic, such as Shirley Temple, had great difficulty succeeding in Hollywood as an adult, with their careers effectively over by the time they reached adulthood. Child actors may or may not enjoy the fame bestowed upon them so early in life, but their fame has almost always come at a cost, especially since it has traditionally been difficult for audiences to disassociate them from their early roles.

On the other hand, the life of Elizabeth Taylor bears little in common with the paradigm of the troubled child star. After arriving in the United States at the age of 9, Taylor was indoctrinated into the life of the Hollywood studio system shortly after child stars Judy Garland and Mickey Rooney, but while Garland suffered great trauma at the hands of the studio system, Taylor's early experience in Hollywood represented the flip side of the coin. Groomed for a life in Hollywood by her zealous mother, Taylor enjoyed her life in the motion picture industry and reveled in the privileged lifestyle and opportunities she enjoyed by virtue of her profession.

Acting supplied her with a lavish lifestyle and, more importantly for her, constant attention. From an early age, Taylor displayed a vociferous love for living in the public eye.

Another difference separating her from other child stars is that Taylor was able to successfully transition from child star to major adult actress; in fact, her fame only escalated as she grew into adulthood. In many ways, Taylor enjoyed being in the public spotlight and living the lifestyle of the rich and famous, and her personal life very much resembled a performance suitable for Hollywood. Taylor faced great adversity throughout her life, including being married on eight different occasions to seven different spouses and fighting battles with weight and drug addiction. Still, while many actors grow resentful of public attention, even during her moments of personal struggle Taylor thrived on public attention and enjoyed a mutually adoring relationship with the American public. She was a creature of the studio system, yet she maintained a dynamic with the public that deviated sharply from the norms of child actors.

This book examines the life and career of Elizabeth Taylor, putting the spotlight on Taylor's child roles and her adult films, and the relationship between the two main stages of her career. Of course, it also documents the notorious elements of her personal life as well. Along with pictures of important people, places, and events, you will learn about Elizabeth Taylor like never before.

Elizabeth Taylor and Richard Burton: A Romance Made and Broken in Hollywood

About Charles River Editors

Introduction

   Chapter 1: Burton's Childhood in Wales

   Chapter 2: From London to the United States

   Chapter 3: Growing Up in Hollywood

   Chapter 4: All The World's a Stage or Screen

   Chapter 5: A Weird Cycle

   Chapter 6: Superstardom

   Chapter 7: The Marriage of the Century

   Chapter 8: Living, Loving and Working Together

   Chapter 9: Making Rubbish

   Chapter 10: The Image as Epitaph

   Chapter 11: Taylor's Later Years

Bibliography

Chapter 1: Burton's Childhood in Wales

"As Lee Marvin says, who gives a shit? We're born, we come staggering out the womb, we come searching for death. My father was a Welsh miner, a remarkable man. Tough, powerful. Obese. Short. I come from an enormous family - thirteen children. My eldest sister was having a baby. I didn't understand it. I said, 'Will she be all right? Will she live?' My father - he was massively drunk - was worried too. 'Never mind,' he said, 'we're all dying.' He talked like an angel. 'Even your growing pains are reaching into oblivion.'" - Richard Burton

Richard Walter Jenkins was born on November 10, 1925, in Pontrhydyfen, Neath Port Talbot, Wales. He was the 12th child of his father, Richard, Sr., a hard-working and hard-drinking coal miner who occasionally escaped the stress of providing for a wife and (eventually) 13 children by going on gambling sprees. According to Richard, "He looked very much like me ...he was pockmarked, devious, and smiled a great deal when he was in trouble. He was, also, a man of extraordinary eloquence, tremendous passion, great violence."

Richard never knew his mother, Edith Maude, because she died in childbirth when he was only two years old. Instead, he was mostly raised by his older sister, Cecilia, who had married and made a home of her own before his birth. Like their father, Cecilia's husband, Elfed, was a miner, and Richard remained close to his surrogate parents for the rest of his life, later saying that Cecilia was "more mother to me than any mother could have been… I was immensely proud of her…she felt all tragedies except her own." In addition to Cecilia, Richard was also close to his brother, Ifor, who was also an adult when Richard was born. Ifor was a steadying influence in Richard's life and "ruled the household with the proverbial firm hand." Like most young men his age, Ifor worked in a coal mine and played on the rugby field; he taught Richard to hate the former and love the latter.

As a young man, Richard would prefer playing rugby to any other activity, but he was also a good student, with a particular aptitude for language and the stories of his people. He was also renowned for his memory, a skill that would stand him in good stead when he began to have to learn lines. However, learning lines for a play was the farthest thing from his mind at that time, as he would later admit, "I would rather have played for Wales at Cardiff Arms Park than Hamlet at the Old Vic."

In 1937, Richard's intelligence and hard work earned him a scholarship to the Port Talbot Secondary School, but it would be a mistake to credit his success in school to a goody-two-shoes wholesomeness. Though he did embrace many of the teachings of the local Presbyterian Church he attended, he also started smoking when he was just 8 years old and began drinking a few years later. To support his new habits, he worked before school delivering newspapers and after school delivering horse manure.

As Richard got older, he came under the influence of Philip H. Burton, the head teacher at his local upper school and a significant influence on his young life. So close were they that Burton even looked into adopting his young charge, and he later called Richard "my son to all intents and purposes. I was committed to him." However, Richard was not quite old enough, just shy of the 20 years age difference that the law demanded between adoptive parents and children. Nonetheless, Philip was the one who recognized Richard's acting talent and encouraged him to appear in the school production of *The Apple Cart*. Richard impressed everyone with both his acting and singing skill, though anyone who ever heard his deep bass voice on screen would probably be shocked to learn that he won a prize for best boy soprano.

Although he always looked up to Burton and would later take his surname as his own, Richard was not sufficiently interested in school to stay after he turned 16. Instead, he went to work for the co-operative committee, a World War II era organization that oversaw rationing supplies to the civilian population. He considered going into the church, either as a minister or a choir director, and he was also interesting in professional boxing. Eventually, Richard joined the Port Talbot Air Squadron, and while in training, he ran into Burton again. By this time, his former teacher had become a commander in the Air Training Corps, and Burton recruited Richard for the camp's drama group. The head of the group, Leo Lloyd, despite only being an amateur performer, managed to instill in Richard some of the basic principles of acting. Richard was his star pupil, and Burton again expressed an interest in his future, going so far as to make him his ward.

Burton also persuaded Richard to graduate from school, and once back in the classroom, Richard soon learned the benefits of being the oldest boy in the class, namely that he was more attractive than ever to girls. He also learned that he had more self-discipline than most of his classmates and, by now, a deeper speaking and singing voice. Meanwhile, Burton continued to tutor Richard in both scholastic subjects and acting skills, as well as take him up into the Welsh mountains and have the young man read *Henry V* aloud. Burton would then begin walking away from him, insisting that Richard continue to make himself heard without shouting. This led Richard to develop the deep and distinct speaking voice that would later help make him famous.

In 1943, Richard Burton enrolled in Exeter College at Oxford, where he remained for six months as part of a special program designed for those preparing to enter the military. During that time, he continued honing his acting skills by appearing in one of William Shakespeare's lesser known plays, *Measure for Measure*, in 1944, as well as *Druid's Rest*. Emlyn Williams, who wrote *Druid's Rest*, would subsequently become one of his mentors, and though the play was panned, Burton's role was praised: "In a wretched part, Richard Burton showed exceptional ability." He would later say that the praise he received for his role in that play was what drove him to pursue acting as a career. He also starred as Professor Higgins in a production of *Pygmalion* put on at the local YMCA, as well as perform some radio work for the BBC.

Williams

In addition to his assigned studies, Burton quickly demonstrated a voraciously appetite for Shakespeare. He made it a practice to always have a copy of one of the bard's plays in hand, and he devoted much of his time to memorizing large chunks of their dialogue. Before long, friends learned that no matter what line they might throw out from a play, Burton could pick up at that point and quote a number of lines after it. He would later admit:

> "I'm a reader, you know. I was corrupted by Faust. And Shakespeare. And [Marcel] Proust. And [Ernest] Hemingway. But mostly I was corrupted by Dylan Thomas. Most people see me as a rake, womanizer, boozer and purchaser of large baubles. I'm all those things depending on the prism and the light. But mostly I'm a reader. Give me Agatha Christie for an hour and I'm happy as a clam. The house in Celigny someday will cave in under its own weight from the books. I hope I'm there when it does. One hundred six years old. Investigating the newest thriller from [John] le Carré or a new play from Tennessee Williams."

Burton also sharpened his brain by doing crossword puzzles and reading histories and biographies. He would remain passionate about the written and spoken word for the rest of his life, once famously saying, "The only thing in life is language. Not love. Not anything else."

Chapter 2: From London to the United States

"It's not the having, it's the getting." – Elizabeth Taylor

Elizabeth Taylor's entry into the world on February 27, 1932 could not have been less glamorous, and one of the great ironies of her life is that when she was born, she was alarmingly ugly. She was born with a condition known as hypertrichosis, which left her face covered with a thin coating of black facial hair (Bret). Every bit as disconcerting was the fact that her eyes were closed shut for a full 10 days following her birth. But ultimately, symptoms lasted just three months, after which Taylor grew into an alarmingly pretty child. Given the ultra-glamorous physique she would later have, and the fact that sickness became a fundamental part of her life story, it was both fitting and ironic that she had the illness. As she grew older, Elizabeth would grow exceptionally savvy in using her own issues to both raise awareness and keep herself in the public eye. In this regard, while one might assume that illness would render someone less glamorous, Taylor possessed a rare talent for using it to her own advantage and transition from illness to health that occurred immediately after being born paralleled many similar events that occurred later in life.

Although her parents were not British, Elizabeth was born at Heathwood, her parents' home in suburban London. She joined her older brother Howard, who was born in 1929, and there would be no other siblings. Elizabeth's middle name was Rosemond, and both her first name and middle name were chosen in homage to her father's mother. Her parents, Francis Lenn Taylor and Sara Sothern, married in 1926 and moved to London around the end of the decade. Though they lived a comfortable, somewhat upscale existence in London, they were actually humble Midwesterners who fell into a fortuitous set of circumstances that facilitated their upward mobility. In fact, at the time of their marriage, the pairing of Francis and Sara was a bizarre one and there was every reason to expect that it would be short-lived.

Francis Taylor grew up in a relatively humble, Presbyterian Midwestern family in Springfield, Illinois, before his family subsequently moved to Arkansas, Kansas. In Kansas, his family ran an express mail and messenger company, but his uncle, Howard Young, was a millionaire and owned an art dealership. Before opening the art gallery, he had first amassed a fortune owning a business retouching family photographs, benefitting from the meteoric American obsession with pictures. When Francis came of age, Young offered his nephew a position with the dealership, giving him the opportunity to prove himself as an art dealer, an industry that held immense potential for wealth.

Francis Taylor

Meanwhile, Sara's family was German and her maiden name was Warmbrodt. Well into her 20s, Sara maintained ambitions of becoming famous in her own right as a stage actress. Her family did not have much money, but Sara was driven to advance farther in life, something that would actually be instrumental in pushing her daughter to stardom. Sara's father, a German immigrant, was trained as an engineer but worked as a foreman-manager at a laundry company (Walker). Like her future husband, Sara was raised in Arkansas City, Kansas, but she did not marry Francis until the age of 30, and though she was ultimately unsuccessful as an actress, she did manage to work as a professional actress during her 20s.

Sara's decision to become an actress was fraught with risk because she quit high school before graduating, effectively limiting her to a life spent either as an actress or as a housewife. Her career as an actress not only demonstrated her interest in show business (which influenced her daughter's entry into the business) but also illuminates how she yearned to escape her Midwestern roots. Upon entering the acting profession, she Anglicized her name to Sara Sothern to make herself more marketable, and she lived as an actress in Los Angeles more than 10 years before the Taylor family moved there during World War II.

Sara Sothern

Sara first made a name for herself in October 1922 when she played the part of the disabled Mary Margaret in *The Fool*, a play written by Channing Pollock. The play began in Los Angeles and enjoyed a prolonged run, as it also toured on Broadway and in the West End of London. While acting, she was placed in the company of very significant actresses, including the famous Russian actress Alla Nazimova. She was unable to use her connections in order to gain significant stage or cinematic roles, but Sara's period as an actress had the significant effect of impressing upon her how to comport herself around people of great influence within the entertainment industry, a skill she would use to great effect when her daughter began acting.

By acting in *The Fool*, Sara resisted the pressures of marriage until the age of 30, but with all of her fame tied to her performance in *The Fool*, she realized that her career was floundering. By 1926, silent cinema was in the process of usurping traditional art forms like the stage and vaudeville theater as the form of American show business *par excellence*. Moreover, one of the oft-overlooked effects of the rising Hollywood film industry was that the movies offered far fewer lucrative roles for women over the age of 30 than the theater. In plays, even middle-age women were able to maintain productive careers, but the young actresses surfacing in the films of directors such as D.W. Griffith created a fundamental shift toward preferring particularly young women.

Furthermore, since Sara was already 30 years old, she was increasingly viewed as an old maid, reaching an age where it would become far more difficult to find a spouse (Kelley). In light of these circumstances, it became clear that Sara Sothern needed to find a husband, and it was in this context that the relationship between her and Francis developed. When Sara and Francis met, it was immediately clear that Sara would need to terminate her career. Not only was it culturally expected that women would give birth and raise children, but Sara's career was not lucrative enough to support a family anyhow.

By this time, Francis was rising through the ranks of his uncle's company, and he was allowed to travel the world in search of artworks. After the couple married, they traveled Europe in search of artworks to purchase, spending time in London, Paris, Berlin, and Vienna, with Francis's uncle subsidizing them to stay in expensive luxury hotels (Walker). In an ironic twist of events, Sara was actually able to travel more frequently as a married woman than during her time as an actress.

While traveling the world, Francis proved himself to be adept at recognizing which artworks would be able to command a high profit, and in 1929 he was promoted to operate his uncle's gallery in London. Displaying expert foresight, Howard purchased paintings at bargain prices and then shipped them across the Atlantic to his uncle's gallery in New York City (Heymann). Shortly after arriving in London, he and Sara gave birth to their first child, Elizabeth's brother Howard. Three years followed before Elizabeth was born, and as a result of being born in England with American parents, she enjoyed dual citizenship. By 1932, the Taylors had settled into a comfortable bourgeois existence in London, an entire ocean removed from their Midwestern roots.

The Taylors' move to London was also facilitated by their good friend Victor Cazalet, an influential figure in London society. An immensely wealthy bachelor, Cazalet was a Member of Parliament with strong ties to the London art and theatre arenas. Cazalet was also a prominent homosexual in London, and it is widely believed that he and Francis maintained a longstanding affair that Sara was fully aware of and did not object to. Cazalet remained a close family friend and was named godfather of Elizabeth. He also played a strong role in the Taylors' support for Christian Science, which would grow increasingly pronounced during Elizabeth's childhood.

Cazalet (left) receiving Polish documents from politician Stanislaw Grabski in London.

The Taylors enjoyed life in London, and Elizabeth referred to her time there in glowing terms later in life. After reaching stardom, she published a book, *Elizabeth Taylor's Nibbles and Me*, describing the environment at the family's home in England: "We had people actually coming to see the place and raving about how pretty we had made it. There was a fireplace in every room. It was like going to bed in fairyland with the windows all wide open and the firelight flickering on the ceilings and walls, and outside even at night the birds would still sing." (Taylor 3-4). It's quite likely Elizabeth took great liberties with this description, given that she was a child when it was written, but readers can still gain an understanding for how enjoyable life in England was for Taylor.

Elizabeth's idyllic childhood also included leisurely activities. According to Sara, when she was just 3, Elizabeth and Howard were placed in a prestigious dancing class that saw them receive elite instruction, but it's possible this anecdote was apocryphal and one of many tales fabricated by Sara after Elizabeth had already reached stardom. The Taylors may have been well-to-do, but they were hardly wealthy and could not provide their children with luxuries. Elizabeth unquestionably had a joyous childhood, but because Sara was always yearning for her family to improve their social standing, she fantasized and took constant liberties with the truth. To this end, Kitty Kelley contends, "Like an antebellum lady with a swansdown fan, Sara Taylor hid her driving ambition behind a soft-spoken façade. A diminutive woman, she spoke with honey-dripping sweetness. She called her husband 'Daddy,' her daughter 'my angel,' and her son 'my sweet lambie pie.' Everyone else was simply 'my dear.'" (2). This description conveys the syrupy sensibility Sara exuded, but also the highly manufactured way in which she comported herself. Sara did not learn such mannerisms while growing up in Kansas, and it's fair to say she remained an actress even after retiring from the stage.

Elizabeth Taylor as a young girl

Chapter 3: Growing Up in Hollywood

"Success is a great deodorant." – Elizabeth Taylor

Despite her mother's narrative, Elizabeth had a relatively normal upbringing in England, and she began her education at the Byron House in Highgate, a region of North London. It was not until the Spring of 1939 that her life truly changed, when the onset of World War II compelled Cazalet to pay for Sara and the children to take a boat to the United States. While the family found residence in America, Francis finalized the closure of the gallery in London and prepared to open a new one in the Los Angeles area.

While on board the ship west, Elizabeth watched her first film, *The Little Princess* (1939), which fittingly starred the reigning queen of child stars, Shirley Temple. Sara and the children arrived in New York City, where they stayed for a brief while, but with no job prospects or permanent residence planned in New York, the family then moved across the country, arriving in Pasadena, California. Relocating to California had the benefit of placing Elizabeth in closer proximity to the Hollywood studios, but the primary impetus for moving to the West Coast was so that the family could live with Sara's uncle, who operated a chicken ranch. The family remained there for nearly a full year, waiting for Francis to arrive and set up his business, and after that was finalized, the family moved to Los Angeles, purchasing a bungalow at Pacific Palisades. For his gallery, Francis rented a suite at the Chateau Elysee Hotel (Bret).

Elizabeth and Howard were placed in a local school near Hollywood, restoring a sense of permanence that had been absent for the past year. During the first year in Los Angeles, Elizabeth's life remained relatively quiet, but Sara continued to harbor great ambitions for her children. As David Bret notes, the same high aspirations she had while living in London were simply transplanted to Hollywood: "Sara had always counted on one or both of her children to provide meal tickets for the future. She had infiltrated London society, working her way into parties and receptions if invitations had not been forthcoming, hoping that Elizabeth or Howard might marry appropriately and elevate the Taylors to the upper classes, where Sara was convinced they belonged." (19).

Having arrived in Hollywood, the family was far from affluent, but Sara no longer had to dream about the possibility that one of her children might marry into wealth. In a climate in which child actors were more popular than ever, Sara could now envision a far quicker path to upward mobility than when the family lived in London. In an effort to receive greater exposure to the Hollywood elite, she convinced her husband to relocate his gallery to the Beverly Hills Hotel on Sunset Boulevard (Bret).

In 1941, Elizabeth received her first opportunity to audition for Hollywood studios, with screen tests for both Universal and Metro-Goldwyn-Mayer. The audition for MGM was particularly prestigious since it was performed for Louis B. Mayer, the (in)famous head of the studio. The

MGM test occurred first, and Sara ensured that she and her child were well-prepared to make a positive impression. Kitty Kelley explained, "For the audition at MGM, Sara dressed Elizabeth in a ruffled pinafore and patent-leather Mary Janes. She also carefully dressed herself. To simulate the silk stockings she could not afford, she rubbed suntan lotion on her legs and drew a dark seam with an eyebrow pencil. Before leaving the house, she sat Elizabeth down with her Christian Science prayer book and instructed her to think good thoughts. They repeated this routine a week later when Elizabeth auditioned at Universal." (Kelley 4).

Louis B. Mayer

The preparation for the screen tests left nothing to chance and revealed the extreme extent to which Sara coached her daughter. That said, Sara's advice was successful, and Elizabeth received offers from both studios. Even though Mayer did not care for her voice, he offered her a contract for $100 per week, to be renewed every six months. With an offer from MGM already on the table, Sara shrewdly played one studio against the other, resulting in an offer from Universal for $200 per week. The offer from Universal was accepted, and Elizabeth Taylor became officially employed as an actress at just 9 years old.

The reasons for why Universal hired Elizabeth Taylor remain a bit unclear. The studio already had a glut of child actors, in light of the bidding war initiated by Elizabeth's mother, it's conceivable that Universal simply wanted to keep the young actress away from MGM, which already employed Judy Garland. In any event, while Universal may well have been impressed by Taylor at the time she was hired, their impression of her cooled after watching her act. Especially noticeable was the fact that Taylor simply had yet to receive any manner of vocal training. Without being able to sing, it was difficult to thrive as a child star; the careers of Judy Garland and Shirley Temple are just two famous examples of the manner in which a skilled singing voice was an unofficial prerequisite for starring in Hollywood as a child. Furthermore, as Kitty Kelley explains, the young Elizabeth Taylor was unable to compensate for this deficiency in other areas: "Universal felt she didn't look as if she could ever be a star. She didn't have dimples like Shirley Temple. She couldn't sing like Judy Garland. She couldn't dance like Jane Powell. She couldn't cry like Margaret O'Brien" (Kelley 4-5).

After one screen test, a casting director asserted, "The kid has nothing." He further complained, "Her eyes are too old, she doesn't have the face of a child." In fact, a lot of people in the industry thought Elizabeth looked too old, as biographer Alexander Walker noted: "There was something slightly odd about Elizabeth's looks, even at this age – an expression that sometimes made people think she was older than she was. She already had her mother's air of concentration. Later on, it would prove an invaluable asset. At the time, it disconcerted people who compared her unfavorably with Shirley Temple's cute bubbling innocence or Judy Garland's plainer and more vulnerable juvenile appeal."

On top of that, in an interview with Rolling Stone in the '80s, Taylor explained that she had never truly been taught how to act:

> "I have never had an acting lesson in my life. But I've learned, I hope, from watching people like Spencer Tracy, Marlon Brando, Montgomery Clift, Jimmy Dean — all people who were finely tuned and educated in the art of acting. They were my education. I found quite early on that I couldn't act as a puppet — there would be something pulling my strings too hard — and that I did my best work by being guided, not by being forced. And I suppose that really is just the child in me — wanting to be allowed to grow and develop at my instinctual sort of pace. If you describe me as an actress, you'd have to say that I wasn't a distinctive actress as actresses go, because I'm certainly not a polished technician."

Universal ultimately gave Taylor a scant three days of acting on *There's One Born Every Minute* (1942), a short 60-minute film that served as Elizabeth's screen debut. Shortly after the stint was completed, however, Universal terminated Taylor's contract. Less than one year after joining the studio, she was already unemployed.

Even though Elizabeth Taylor was still just a child, her earnings with Universal went a long way toward subsidizing the family, because World War II had a negative impact on the earnings of Francis's studio. The Taylors were required to place half of their daughter's earnings in a trust fund that Elizabeth could not access until she was 21, but Francis and Sara spent almost all of the remaining funds on their home. In order to pay the family bills, it was thus necessary for Elizabeth to secure employment immediately after getting dropped from Universal.

Fortunately, Francis had served as an air raid warden with Sam Marx, a prominent producer with MGM. Through Marx, Francis heard that MGM was in the process of looking for a child star to play the role of Priscilla in *Lassie Come Home* (1943), the granddaughter of the rich Duke who purchases the eponymous dog. Not only did Taylor benefit from her father's connections with the famous producer, but also aiding her profile was that Louis B. Mayer was fond of England and British actors (Kelley). Before Sara wanted her daughter to sign a contract with Mayer, she famously wanted a sign that it was the right choice. Biographer Alexander Walker described how the decision was reached:

> "Was there a divine plan for her? Mrs. Taylor took her old script for The Fool, in which she had played the scene of the girl whose faith is answered by a miracle cure. Now she asked Elizabeth to read her own part, while she read the lines of the leading man. She confessed to weeping openly. She said, 'There sat my daughter playing perfectly the part of the child as I, a grown woman, had tried to do it. It seemed that she must have been in my head all those years I was acting'"

Taylor was given the role, as well as a long-term contract with MGM at the start of 1943, and the impact of *Lassie Come Home* on her career cannot be overstated. Having lived in London for the first nine years of her life, she was a natural fit for the role of the young girl who facilitates Lassie's escape from Scotland. The film was a major commercial triumph; a relatively early example of Technicolor, it benefitted from the novelty of color film and was appropriately nominated for Academy Awards for Cinematography and Color. Off the movie set, Elizabeth established what would become a close friendship with her male co-star, Roddy McDowell. She was still earning just $100 per week, but the film gave her the national exposure she needed to truly elevate her status within the cutthroat environment of Hollywood cinema. While it is true that there were fewer child actors than adult ones, it was still necessary for child stars to carve out a niche for themselves, and with *Lassie Come Home*, Elizabeth Taylor proved that she was ideally suited for dramatic, tearjerker films.

Taylor in *Lassie Come Home*

The success of *Lassie Come Home* fundamentally altered Elizabeth Taylor's life. She was placed in a school that was structured to accommodate her acting schedule, and she couldn't help but become increasingly aware of her celebrity status. Years later, she would note that becoming famous as a child had a fundamental impact on how she self-identified:

> "From the age of nine I began to see myself as two separate people: Elizabeth Taylor the person, and Elizabeth Taylor the commodity. I saw the difference between my image and my real self. Sometimes [as a child] when I was out riding, I would pretend to be part of a fantasy high school or campus scene, but a few hours later I would be back on the set creating the public Elizabeth Taylor." (Papa 23).

Elizabeth was thus faced with the challenge of distinguishing between her private and public selves. Even though she maintained interests outside of Hollywood, she was not allowed to pursue off-screen activities for long before she was required to appear on the movie set.

Lassie Come Home was instrumental in raising Elizabeth to stardom, but the two films she appeared in following her breakthrough film were hardly major performances for her. The first featured her in *Jane Eyre* (1944), a big budget adaptation of the famous Bronte novel. The film was not actually produced by MGM but instead by 20th Century Fox, with Elizabeth loaned by her parent studio to appear in the film in an uncredited role. Taylor's next film, *The While Cliffs of Dover* (1944), similarly relegated her to a minor, uncredited appearance. The film accomplished virtually nothing in furthering her career, but it reunited her with Roddy McDowell, and the on-location shooting in England gave her the opportunity to return to her roots. She continued to be paid an amount that was hardly insignificant by the standards of Depression-era America, but it would not be until after her following film that she began to enter the highest ranks of the MGM pantheon.

If *Lassie Come Home* was Elizabeth Taylor's first breakthrough, it paled in comparison with her next major film, *National Velvet* (1944). The genesis for the role occurred in 1943, when Pandro Berman, the film's producer, identified her as the leading actress. However, at that time, Taylor was undersized, even for her age, and Berman was forced to either delay production or select another actress. Surprisingly, he was so insistent on featuring Taylor that he delayed the production substantially and waited until 1944 before shooting commenced. The film was an enormous production, in part because of MGM's decision to pair Taylor with the ever-popular Mickey Rooney, who had recently outgrown his status as the preeminent child actor. With a budget of $2.77 million, there was significant risk in the film, but Pandro Berman had a number of things working in his favor. The movie starred two of the most famous child stars, and the script was borrowed from the famous novel of the same name by Enid Bagnold.

Taylor in *National Velvet*

Shooting *National Velvet* was a great joy for Taylor, largely due to the plot of the film. Starring in the eponymous role, Elizabeth relished the opportunity to play the young jockey who wins a horse and rises to fame. A passionate animal lover, Elizabeth enjoyed taking riding lessons in preparation for the role, and she would ride horses throughout her adult life as well. Biographer Alexander Walker noted the effects the film had on viewers, writing, "Its enormous popularity rubs off on to its heroine because she expresses, with the strength of an obsession, the aspirations of people—people who have never seen a girl on horseback, or maybe even a horse race for that matter—who believe that anything is possible ... A philosophy of life, in other words ... a film which ... has acquired the status of a generational classic..."

At the same time, however, as Elizabeth moved further and further into the MGM family, the status of her biological family began to fall into disarray. In particular, Francis and Howard became secluded from Elizabeth and her mother, and a marriage that had never been particularly intimate became even more fractured. Francis grew angry at the circumstances his daughter was placed in during the film, which included Elizabeth needing to wear braces. It was originally determined that Taylor would shave her hair for the part, but Francis intervened, and she was eventually allowed to wear a wig. Still, for all of the discomfort involved in watching his daughter helplessly from the sidelines, there was little Francis could do to change the circumstances. Referring to Francis, Kitty Kelley explains that Elizabeth began to disregard him in favor of her co-star from *National Velvet*: "his position as husband, father, and head of the household was slowly eroding. That year Elizabeth bought two Valentines. One she gave to her father, and forgot to sign it. The other went to her movie father, Donald Crisp. On it she wrote: *"From your littlest daughter with love, Velvet.'"* (12). In a sense the anecdote reveals the challenges of expecting a child actress to distinguish between her life on set and off set, but that episode exemplified how Francis became a less important figure in Elizabeth Taylor's life as she grew older.

National Velvet was so successful that MGM immediately signed Taylor to a long-term contract that paid her double what she had been making. As an additional reward for the popularity of the film, Louis B. Mayer also gave Taylor a $15,000 bonus, in addition to a skilled interior designer. In short, she received the full-fledged star treatment, a surprising development in light of Mayer's penurious reputation. By the mid-1940s, Taylor earned $30.000, with one-third of this salary turned over to her parents.

Similar to many of the other MGM starlets, Mayer was treated as a paternal figure of authority for Elizabeth, and establishing such a dynamic with Louis B. Mayer meant that an actress occupied a position near the top of the MGM hierarchy. Since Elizabeth's rise to fame coincided with the onset of World War II, she was forced to donate 10% of her salary to pay for war bonds and stamps, a patriotic gesture imposed by MGM, but nevertheless, by the time she was a teenager, Elizabeth Taylor had acted in a small number of films and enjoyed a life of great luxury, even though she hadn't reached the apex of her popularity. And given the sacrifices others were making during the war, Taylor was most fortunate, as she did not have to part ways with anyone in her immediate family: "Elizabeth had been insulated from the war. Her father had been too old to enlist and her brother was too young. Mickey Rooney was one of the few persons she knew to actually go into the armed services...Although she was thirteen years old when President Roosevelt died, his death had little impact on her, partly because her parents were such staunch Republicans that they totally ignored the nation's intense grief." (Kelley 16).

In essence, during her upbringing Elizabeth was entirely removed from the turmoil that afflicted the nation. Later in life she would become quite active in championing the causes of underrepresented groups, despite forever retaining her parents' right-wing political stances, but in the '40s she was at an age where politics meant nothing.

Taylor in 1944

Perhaps the greatest challenge facing child actors involves how to follow up their early successes, particularly as their body develops. Just as adult actresses often lose popularity as they reach middle age, child stars have historically had great difficulty maintaining success as they transition into young adulthood.

MGM handled Elizabeth carefully, because they were well-aware that she was both a tremendously valuable commodity but also a potentially volatile one due to her age. After *National Velvet*, Elizabeth did not appear in any movies for a year-and-a-half. Taking such an extended absence would be significant even in an adult star, but for a child actor the effect was even more pronounced, as Taylor was growing up quite visibly with each passing year.

Taylor in 1945

Taylor in 1947

However, as Taylor began to grow up, she also became more independent and assertive, just as MGM was trying to control her image more. When asked in an interview whether MGM was like a family, she snapped back:

> "It was like a big extended factory, I'm sorry to say. But if you like being smothered, I guess it was a very productive family. I was nine when I made my first films in Hollywood. I was used from the day I was a child, and utilized by the studio. I was promoted for their pockets. I never felt that they were a haven. I've always been very much my own person. I had my own mother and father — they were my family, not the bloody studio.

> When I was 15 and Louis B. Mayer started screaming at my mother and using swear words that I'd never heard before ('I took you and your f***ing daughter out of the gutter'), I uttered my first swear word and told him that he didn't dare speak to my mother that way, and he and the studio could both go to hell, and that I was never going to go back to his office. And I left my mother there with her eyes shut, and I think she was sort of praying…
>
> I walked out of there in such a fury and in tears, and went to see my old friend and vice-president Benny and he said, "You have to go back." And another vice president came and found me. Now those guys were my buddies, and they said, "Sweetheart you have got to go back and apologize." And I said, "What for? He should apologize to my mother I'm not going back in his office. I meant what I said and I don't care if you fire me now. I don't know where I found the independence. I totally winged it on my own and just took my career, with total knowledge and decision, and threw it out the window. Now I had not a clue how L. B. Mayer — one of the great icons of Hollywood history, and slightly mad, and who was frothing at the mouth in a temper — would take this from a pipsqueak. But I didn't care. I knew that he had done something very wrong. As it turns out they must have wanted or needed me. Otherwise they wouldn't have kept me. But that only has occurred to me in hindsight."

Taylor also tried to avoid aesthetic changes the studio tried to make in an effort to sex up her image, telling the Rolling Stone interviewer:

> "My god, I had black hair — it was photographed blue-black it was so dark — and thick bushy eyebrows. And my mother and father had to stop them from dying my hair and plucking out my eyebrows. The studio even wanted to change my name to Virginia. They tried to get me to create a Joan Crawford mouth when I first began using lipstick at 15. They wanted, you know, Joan Crawford, the '40s and everything. Every movie star, Lana Turner, all of them, painted over their lips: and I'm sure that some of them had perfectly fine, full lips — but thin eyebrows were the fad…and God forbid you do anything individual or go against the fad. But I did. I figured this looks absurd. And I agreed with my dad: God must have had some reason for giving me bushy eyebrows and black hair. I guess I must have been pretty sure of my sense of identity. It was me. I accepted it all my life and I can't explain it. Because I've always been very aware of the inner me that has nothing to do with the physical me."

By the time Taylor returned to the screen in 1946, she was beginning to develop into a young woman, and the next few years were a second phase of sorts for her as a child actress. The first film she appeared in following her hiatus, *Courage of Lassie* (1946), harkened back to her first major film role, but the two films bear little similarities outside of their titles. None of the plotlines from the earlier film are referenced, and this time Taylor plays Kathie Merrick, a teenage girl living on a sheep ranch. Merrick adopts a young Collie, and the narrative involves her losing her dog and finally reconciling with him at the conclusion. One of the more noticeable aspects of *Courage of Lassie* is the way in which it essentially transplants the male-female romance that typically comprised the plot of Hollywood films and applies the romance to the relationship between Elizabeth Taylor's character and her dog. In this regard, Taylor was positioned in a role that remained in the model of the child actress, while at the same time making it possible for audiences to envision her as a romantic heroine. Although *Courage of Lassie* remains considerably less-known than the earlier Lassie film, it is nevertheless significant for its status as an intermediary film bridging Taylor's early child films with her later performances as a female romantic lead.

Following *Courage of Lassie*, MGM had difficulty placing Taylor in roles that were appropriate for her age. Much of this was because the Teen Comedy genre that enjoys great popularity in 21st century Hollywood did not exist in the 1940s, and teenagers simply did not star in many films during that era, particularly if they could not sing or dance, as was the case with Taylor. She was therefore relegated to playing relatively minor roles as a daughter in family melodramas and comedies, essentially reduced to playing spoiled rich girls. The first of these films was *Life with Father* (1947), directed by German expatriate Michael Curtiz, who had already reached great fame with *Casablanca* (1941). Taylor was loaned to Warner Brothers for the film, and the big-budget nature of the production was evident by the stars in the cast, which included Irene Dunne, William Powell, and Zazu Pitts.

Curtiz

The film was neither a big box office success nor a significant milestone in Taylor's career, but the activity off the movie set, which fundamentally altered the family environment. Sara and director Michael Curtiz had an affair, a development that was not particularly surprising considering the fact that she and her husband had never been particularly romantic (Kelley). After learning of the affair, Francis left California with Howard for Wisconsin, where they remained for an extended period. Although they eventually returned, the period was a time of great anguish for Taylor, and she began suffering from a variety of illnesses, including bloodshot eyes. Her sicknesses may well have been legitimate, or they may have been the result of stress. She was predisposed toward falling ill, particularly during times of anguish, but she managed to take the attention she received while sick and use it to stay in the spotlight as well.

Furthermore, Elizabeth had trouble dealing with the unusual nature of her schedule, and the manner in which it affected school and normal activities for a teenager. She explained how her career precluded her from a normal childhood in the Rolling Stone interview:

> "One of the few times I've ever really been happy in my life was when I was a kid before I started acting. With the other kids I'd make up games, play with dolls, pretend games ... As I got more famous—after National Velvet, when I was 12—I still wanted to be part of their lives, but I think in a way they began to regard me as a sort of an oddity, a freak.
>
> I hated school—because it wasn't school. I wanted terribly to be with kids. On the set the teacher would take me by my ear and lead me into the schoolhouse. I would be infuriated; I was 16 and they weren't taking me seriously. Then after about 15 minutes I'd leave class to play a passionate love scene as Robert Taylor's wife."

Due to her lack of schooling and disinterest in the format, 16 year old Elizabeth could only count by using her fingers.

After *Life with Father,* Elizabeth appeared in another film in 1947, *Cynthia,* which returned her to MGM and featured her in another role as a rich teenage girl. The film bore clear parallels with her own life, as she plays a young actress. Over the next few years, she continued to appear in about two films per year, with most of her performances consisting of playing affluent teenage girls. None of the films she appeared in through 1949 played a significant role in expanding her star image, but she did gain experience and acting in the musical *A Date with Judy* (1948), which allowed her to improve her singing voice. Even though Taylor was viewed as an important figure in the MGM lineup of stars, she continued to be cast in a limited range of character roles. In 1948, she was cast in *Julia Misbehaves,* and that was followed by *Little Women* (1949), but neither film brought her out of the realm of the family melodrama.

It was not until *Conspirator* (1949) that Elizabeth appeared in a more adult role, as an American woman who falls in love with a man later discovered to be a Russian spy. Even though Taylor was just 16 years old, she was physically developed enough to convincingly portray her 18-year old character, even while being was far younger than her 30-year old co-star, Robert Taylor.

Elizabeth and Robert Taylor in *Conspirator*

Chapter 4: All The World's a Stage or Screen

"The Robe (1953) was lousy, but an almighty hit. I was dull as ditchwater and an almighty flop. My next film, Prince of Players (1955), was Hollywood's first turkey in Cinemascope - when Cinemascope was new and hotter than a pistol. If I'd been able to buttonhole a couple of relatives and persuade a few of the deluded girls I'd done favors for, I'd still have struggled to rustle up nine lost souls to form a fan club." - Richard Burton

While Taylor was born in London and quickly moved to the U.S., Burton found himself gravitating toward the place of her birth. After graduation, Burton joined the Royal Air Force, but while he had hoped to be a pilot, his eyesight was not good enough, so he became a navigator. In 1946, Philip Burton used his influence with the military to arrange for Richard to be granted sufficient leave to allow him to star in a made-for-TV version of the famous Welsh play *The Corn is Green*. After his official discharge from the RAF in 1947, Richard appeared with

Philip and his idol Dylan Thomas in *In Parenthesis* (1948), and he would always consider that BBC production to be some of his finest work.

Dylan Thomas

By the time Burton left the Air Force, he moved to London as an aspiring actor, and once there, he registered with an acting agency to put out the word that he was available for screen tests and casting calls. His first post-war stage performance was in *Castle Anna* in 1948, after which he starred in *The Last Days of Dolwyn* (1949). Burton's performance was praised for being both "volatile and sensitive", and another critic commented on his "acting fire, manly bearing, and good looks." While making the *Last Days of Dolwyn*, Burton met Sybil Williams, who was also in the movie, and they quickly married in February 1949.

Sybil Williams

In spite of the success of his first movie, Burton still considered himself primarily a stage actor, so he headed back to the London stage to appear in *The Lady's Not for Burning*. After it closed in 1950, he moved on to *A Phoenix Too Frequent* and *The Boy With a Cart* in 1950, as well as *The Legend of Lovers* in 1951. The former proved pivotal in his career, as it brought him to the attention of British actor/director Anthony Quayle.

Quayle

Burton also continued to appear in British movies, including *The Woman With No Name* (1950) and *Waterfront* (1950), as well as *Green Grow the Rushes* (1951). British critics soon recognized his talent, with one writing, "He has all the qualifications of a leading man that the British film industry so badly needs at this juncture: youth, good looks, a photogenic face, obviously alert intelligence, and a trick of getting the maximum of attention with a minimum of fuss."

In 1951, Burton appeared in a series of Shakespeare plays performed at the famous Stratford, and much to his delight, Philip Burton showed up to help coach him in his role at Prince Hal in *Henry IV*. This proved to be critically important for Richard, since he was having a difficult time learning to get along with other actors, many of whom outranked him in age and experience. For instance, he often locked horns with Anthony Quayle, who played opposite him as Falstaff. The senior actor had little patience for the upstart's often distracting interest in drinking and story-telling. Despite the distractions, however, Richard's performance ended up surpassing everyone's expectations, with one critic beaming, "His playing of Prince Hal turned interested speculation to awe almost as soon as he started to speak; in the first intermission local critics stood agape in the lobbies."

As Burton made a name for himself, he found himself rubbing shoulders with other acting luminaries, such as John Gielgud and Michael Redgrave, and he also met American stars like Humphrey Bogart and Lauren Bacall, who had come to London to make a movie. They were both impressed with him, and, according to Bacall, "Bogie loved him. We all did. You had no alternative." Of course, it didn't hurt that Bogart had finally found someone who could match him drink for drink at the local pub. Indeed, Burton was already drinking more than he should, and he began drinking even more following the death of his beloved friend Dylan Thomas in 1953. Those were dark days for the young actor, who was always looking for someone to respect and emulate, much as he should have been able to respect his father. However, Burton had little time to dwell on the past; by this time, his future was rushing at him at a high speed.

Bogart and Bacall

When Bogart returned to Hollywood, he wasted no time contacting producer Alexander Korda and telling him about Burton. His praises rang true and were consistent with what Korda could gather from other sources, so Korda invited the young actor to come to Hollywood and try his hand with American film making. Burton accepted and was soon on his way, both figuratively and literally, to Hollywood stardom.

Korda

Burton's first role as part of his five year contract with Korda was opposite Olivia de Havilland in *My Cousin Rachel* (1952), which featured de Havilland as a woman suspected of murdering her husband. Ironically, Korda did not make this movie; instead, he loaned Burton to Paramount Studios, which paid Korda $100,000 to use Burton in this movie and two more. Of course, it had greatly helped that Burton was favored for the role by Daphne du Maurier, who wrote the novel the film was based on. The movie was a big hit and the perfect introduction for Burton to the American public. According to one critic, "...it is really Richard Burton, an English actor new to Hollywood, who gives the most fetching performance as the young gentleman of the doubts and storms. Mr. Burton, lean and handsome, is the perfect hero of Miss du Maurier's tale. His outbursts of ecstasy and torment are in the grand romantic style." The role won Burton a Golden Globe Award for New Star of the Year and earned him an Oscar nomination for Best Supporting Actor.

Burton got along well with James Mason, who starred with him in *Desert Rats* (1953). In fact, Mason liked the new kid on the block so much that he took Burton under his wing and introduced him to other Hollywood stars. Before long, Burton was partying with Judy Garland and Stewart Granger and sitting next to Greta Garbo at dinner parties as Cole Porter played the piano. It was at one of these parties that he first met his future wife; but if he was smitten, Taylor was not; she later commented that, upon meeting Burton, her first impression was that "he was rather full of himself. I seem to remember that he never stopped talking, and I had given him the cold fish eye."

Burton in *Desert Rats*

James Mason in *Northwest by Northwest*

Fortunately, critics liked Burton better than Taylor initially did. For example, one wrote, "Mr. Burton's electric portrayal of the hero nullifies a cardboard assignment and at times almost makes 'The Desert Rats' more than a plain…apology." And Burton's next performance in *The*

Robe (1953) earned him another Oscar nomination, this time for Best Actor, as well as critical praise. One review observed, "Richard Burton, the young English actor who distinguished himself previously…is stalwart, spirited and stern as the arrogant Roman tribune who has command of the crucifixion of Christ and who eventually becomes a passionate convert through an obsession about the Savior's robe."

Burton in *The Robe*

The Robe was a pivotal film for several reasons. Not only was it the first movie filmed in Cinemascope, it also launched a new era for Biblical films and led to the making of such classics as *Ben-Hur* (1959) and *The Ten Commandments* (1956). On a personal level, it eventually led to Burton signing a million dollar contract with Darryl F. Zanuck and Fox Studios. Nevertheless,

Burton still preferred the stage to the screen, once saying, "I have always felt that the camera hasn't liked me. I'm a stage animal. I have to be big and loud, and the camera needs you to be small and naturalistic and subtle; much more naturalistic. I'm as subtle as a buffalo stampede."

Thus, when not in Hollywood, Burton was back in London at the Old Vic theatre, where he appeared in *Coriolanus* and *Hamlet* in 1953. He also played Iago and Othello, but the one role that he was reluctant to try was the most famous: Hamlet. At that time, only the best of the best had ever successfully starred as the troubled prince, and even his friend Humphrey Bogart didn't think that he was up to it, warning Burton, "I never knew a man who played Hamlet who didn't die broke." Still, there was one man who thought he could do it, and that was enough. Philip Burton agreed to coach him for the role, and, with Claire Bloom playing Ophelia, the play finally opened. Unfortunately, the reviews were not great, and Burton came to believe he never should have taken the role in the first place.

In an effort to lick his wounds, Burton next tried his hand at radio work by narrating *Under Milk Wood* in 1954. It was a very personal experience for him, since it had been written by Dylan Thomas shortly before his death, and the production was a type of fundraiser for Thomas' widow and children. Neither Burton nor any of the other actors received any payment for their roles, and all the royalties from the production went to Thomas' family.

Burton returned to moviemaking to star in *Prince of Players* (1955) and *The Rains of Ranchipur* (1955), and though neither of these movies were very memorable, the latter did earn his some critical acclaim, with one review noting, "Credit Richard Burton, as Dr. Safti, and Eugenie Leontovich, as the Maharani, who looks like a tiny, exquisite Hindu figurine, with truly sensitive, dignified and restrained portrayals that often tower above the lines they speak." Still, he was happiest on stage, so he went back to the stage to star in *Henry V* in 1955, and his performance was so strong that Kenneth Tynan publically proclaimed Burton "the natural successor to [Laurence] Olivier."

Chapter 5: A Weird Cycle

Burton and Yvonne Furneaux performing a production of *Wuthering Heights* in 1958.

"Actors go through cycles - remarkable, weird cycles. There was one period from 1956 to 1961 or so when I couldn't do anything right. My voice went foul, my luck was bad, I chose badly. I thought I had lost what I had, and I nearly retired right then and there." - Richard Burton

When he returned to Hollywood, Burton was happy to learn that he had been loaned to United Artists to star in the title role of *Alexander the Great* (1956). On a personal level, he was pleased that he would again be playing opposite Claire Bloom, with whom he had begun an affair while working on *Hamlet*. Burton also liked the story and the script, so he had high hopes for the film.

Unfortunately, he was in for a disappointment, as critics panned the movie and the public stayed away. He would later admit, "None of my films has done me any good. I know all epics are awful, but I thought *Alexander the Great* might be the first good one. I was wrong. They cut it about - played down to the audience. I say if the audience doesn't understand, let 'em stay ignorant."

Claire Bloom

Again disappointed with Hollywood, Burton returned to the stage to star in *Othello* in 1956, and 1957 proved to be a pivotal year in Burton's personal life. In January, his father died suddenly from a cerebral hemorrhage, a death made even more tragic by the fact that he had been estranged from his youngest son for years after refusing to accept his career choices. According to Burton, it was a prejudice born out of homophobia: "My father said all actors were homosexuals. That is nonsense, of course...I was a homosexual once, but not for long. But I tried it. It didn't work so I gave it up." Still, because of this and other reasons, he refused to attend his father's funeral, allowing their mutual animosity to continue past the grave.

Not long after his father's death, Burton made the difficult decision to move his family to Switzerland and become a permanent resident there. His reasons were strictly financial; by this time, his earnings from making movies had placed him in such a high tax bracket that he was keeping less than half of what he made each year, so moving to Switzerland made sense. On a brighter note, his first daughter Kate was born in September. One might speculate that getting pregnant was an attempt by Sybil to hold on to her philandering husband, but it would be hard to know for sure. Ironically, Burton's future wife, Elizabeth Taylor, also gave birth to a daughter, Liza Todd, the previous month. Burton would later adopt the little girl after her father, producer Mike Todd, was killed in a plane crash.

However, things were not going so well from a professional standpoint. In fact, at one point that year, Burton told a reporter, "My real interest in life is the theatre, and I think I've shot my bolt in London as far as the classical roles are concerned." He later added, "I've played all the parts I think I can play, and one or two that I should have given a miss. But there is nothing left until I'm older and can play parts like Lear." Still, he tried his hand in both the stage and screen versions of *Sea Wife* (1957), as well as the play *Time Remembered* (1957), with the latter earning him his first Tony nomination.

Burton then starred in the less-than-memorable movie *Bitter Victory* (1957) before starring as Jimmy Porter in *Look Back in Anger* (1958). Once again, he co-starred with Bloom, allowing them a discreet cover for their romance, and though most critics disagreed with him, Burton liked his performance in the film. He wrote in a letter to Philip Burton, "I promise you that there isn't a shred of self-pity in my performance. I am for the first time ever looking forward to seeing a film in which I play". Indeed, his role earned him nominations for a BAFTA Award for Best British Actor and a Golden Globe Award for Best Actor in a Motion Picture Drama

In spite of his positive feelings about *Look Back in Anger*, Burton's passion still lay with Shakespeare and the stage. In 1959, he narrated *A Midsummer Night's Dream*, and he also lent his deep voice to the role of Winston Churchill in the World War II documentary *The Valiant Years* (1960). Back in Hollywood, he made the ill-fated moves of agreeing to star in *The Bramble Bush* (1960) and *Ice Palace* (1960), leading him to later complain ruefully, "I played a sex-drenched doctor in *The Bramble Bush*. It was the worst picture I ever made, if you don't count *Ice Palace*. That one was based upon a very weak novel by Edna Ferber. Both pictures for Warner Brothers. Jack L. Warner told the press I had no sex appeal. Then Elizabeth came along. All changed after that. Suddenly, Eddie Fisher didn't have sex appeal. And I did. It's a crazy world for a Welsh coal miner's son born in November 1925."

Meanwhile, Burton was far more focused on what would become his most famous role, that of the legendary King Arthur in Broadway's *Camelot* (1960). His role opposite the exquisite Julie Andrews ultimately won him a Tony Award for Best Actor in a Musical, and he would later say of his Guinevere, "Every man I know who knows her is a little bit in love with her."

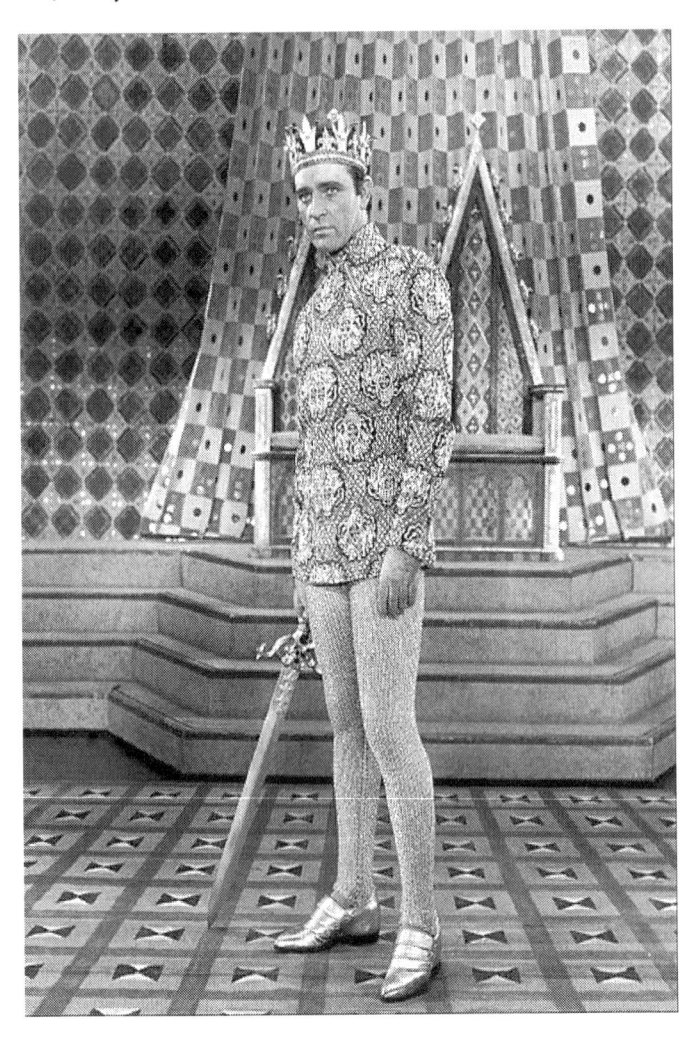

Burton and Andrews in *Camelot*

The classic Broadway production was written by Alan Lerner and directed by Moss Hart, but both men became ill during the show, and their illnesses, coupled with problems coordinating the schedules of their many important actors and show's outrageous length (nearly 5 hours), led to huge headaches for both the investors and participants alike. Ironically, it was within this context that Burton shone the best, maintaining his professionalism and keeping everyone else's spirits up. Lerner himself would later praise Burton's efforts, saying that "he kept the boat from rocking, and Camelot might never have reached New York if it hadn't been for him." His efforts paid off when the show opened to excellent reviews, with one critic raving that Burton "gives Arthur the skillful and vastly appealing performance that might be expected from one of

England's finest young actors."

Not only did Burton get *Camelot* up and going, he and Andrews worked together to keep it running. After a few months, interest in the play began to wane, as most serious fans had already seen it, so to stir up ticket sales, Burton and Andrews made a special appearance on *The Ed Sullivan Show* and sang a charming duet of "What do the Simple Folk Do?" This got ticket sales going again.

One might think that his success with *Camelot* would leave Burton feeling on top of the world, but instead, he fell into something of a depression following its run. In 1962, he told a reporter, "I'm too old. I'm now thirty-six. And I look about 5'2". I'm 5'10" but I look smaller. It's because I'm so wide or my head's too big or something." Of course, just as Burton was talking himself down and it looked like his career was coming to a premature end, it was just about to take off.

Chapter 6: Superstardom

"The problem with people who have no vices is that generally you can be pretty sure they're going to have some pretty annoying virtues." – Elizabeth Taylor

Frustrated with the narrow range of roles she received as a teenager, Taylor expressed an interest in quitting acting altogether in 1948 and being a normal kid, but she was quickly dispelled of the possibility by her mother. Her mother essentially vetoed it and told her, "But you're not a regular child, and thank God for that. You have a responsibility, Elizabeth. Not just to this family, but to the country now, the whole world."

Meanwhile, Taylor remained popular, and MGM never considered releasing her. Nearly as important as managing her career was the necessity of monitoring Taylor's personal life; always notorious for keeping a tight grip over the activities of their stars off the movie set, MGM ensured that Taylor did not become romantically involved with someone who would tarnish her virtuous name, not to mention her status as a virgin. Accordingly, she began dating for the first time in 1948, with her first boyfriend being the clean-cut Glenn Davis, an All-American football player from West Point. Their dates were chaste, characteristically American affairs, including barbecues and touch football, but they were also photographed kissing each other (Kelley). While the relationship was largely fabricated by MGM, Taylor did maintain affection for her first boyfriend, and she was more enthusiastic about Davis than her mother. Fully cognizant that Davis did not come from a wealthy family, Sara expressed immediate disdain for her daughter's boyfriend, while Elizabeth's father Francis appreciated his wholesome values. Regardless, the relationship was forever compromised when Davis was required to enter the service.

Naturally, as she continued to grow older, Taylor's romantic activities didn't slow down, and her subsequent relationships were significantly more high-profile than her first. Rumor had it that eccentric billionaire Howard Hughes, already in his 40s, attempted to court Elizabeth by trying to convince her parents to get her to marry him. Hughes even promised to build Taylor her own studio, but Taylor's response to her parents' prodding was, "Absolutely not. I don't want anything to do with him; I don't care how much money he has."

Elizabeth also dated Bill Pawley, the son of the United States Ambassador to Peru and Brazil. Pawley worked as a pilot in the Air Corps and was 28 at the time he and Taylor met and began dating. Despite the age difference, they got engaged in 1949, but Pawley made it clear that if Taylor married him, she would need to end her career in the interests of raising a family. This stipulation ultimately compelled Elizabeth to end the marriage plans, and the couple separated in 1949.

While her mother has taken a lot of flak for pushing Elizabeth into the business, her decision to forgo a life of comfortable domesticity in favor of pursuing her own career is a reminder of Elizabeth's own ambition, as well as a complex dimension to her personality. Elizabeth's conservative political leanings did not preclude her from shunning a traditional lifestyle, and her career aspirations reveal a progressive mentality that was unusual in the 1940s.

Taylor's third relationship proved to be more enduring, although only slightly; in the fall of 1949, she met Conrad Hilton Jr. (known as Nicky) after being introduced to him at the Paramount studio, and they began dating shortly thereafter. Hilton was the heir to the famous hotel chain, with his wealth estimated at a gaudy $125 million, a fact that Sara appreciated greatly. After a somewhat brief courtship, Hilton proposed to Taylor and they married on May 6, 1950.

Recognizing how lucrative Taylor's romance with Hilton could become, MGM capitalized on the opportunity to turn their famous female star's romance into financial gain and marketed the relationship heavily. By the time her marriage arrangements were finalized, Elizabeth was signed on to star in the romantic comedy *Father of the Bride* (1950), in which she plays a bride whose father has difficulty relinquishing control of her. MGM shrewdly decided to release the film exactly one month after the marriage, knowing full well that audiences would be attracted to both the autobiographical aspects of the film, as well as the opportunity to watch her in her final film as a bachelorette. In addition to promoting the film, MGM supplied Taylor with her wedding dress, and the wedding itself was filmed and released for the public to see. The studio ensured that all of the significant stars of MGM were in attendance, and there were over 700 guests in all.

In a way, it's almost fitting that MGM had such a heavy involvement in the wedding, given the way the studio had exerted control over Elizabeth's life and career. Furthermore, the wedding and even the marriage were practically performances for Taylor and events that helped build her star image.

Elizabeth Taylor and Nicky Hilton

Elizabeth Taylor's wedding footage is well-known and in some respects a film unto itself. Watching the footage, it is difficult to see past the awkwardness of a young woman's wedding being transformed into a pop culture event. At no point during the proceedings does Taylor appear to truly be enjoying herself; in fact, she appears more natural in her films than during her own wedding. Hilton appears slightly more comfortable than Taylor, yet both appear overwhelmed by the magnitude of the event. Still, the crass commercialization of the wedding was merely the first example of a trend that has continued ever since, and Taylor's first wedding was proof that there was no aspect of a celebrity's lifestyle considered too sacred for marketing.

Even though the film is inextricably linked to Taylor's own wedding, *Father of the Bride* was an important film for Taylor and arguably one of the most compelling films she was in. For the only time in her career, Elizabeth was given the opportunity to work with Vincente Minnelli, and Spencer Tracy and Joan Bennett starred as her parents. One of the great ironies of the film is that it was designed to be released in tandem with Taylor's own marriage, and yet the film offers a sensitive critique of marriage in general and the commercialization of consumer culture. In the film, Spencer Tracy's character has difficulty relinquishing control of his daughter and expresses discomfort toward the extreme expenses involved in marriage. While the film is not outwardly opposed to marriage, it forces the viewer to consider the absurdity of spending a lot of money on an occasion that should ostensibly revolve around a simple expression of love and commitment between two individuals.

Taylor and Tracy in *Father of the Bride*

The marriage between Elizabeth Taylor and Nicky Hilton was treated as a joyous affair by MGM, not to mention Elizabeth's own mother, but it was fraught with difficulty from the start. Unlike Pawley, Hilton was able to accept a wife who worked, but he could not cope with the fact that his wife's fame far exceeded his own. Hilton quickly learned to his chagrin that marrying a famous female actress placed the husband into a position of subordination that deviated from the norm. Out of resentment, Hilton gambled heavily and slept with several other women, behavior that created a public relations nightmare for both Taylor and MGM. Taylor would later say about the marriage, "Then came disillusionment, rude and brutal. I fell off my pink cloud with a thud." Worse yet, Hilton began physically and verbally abusing Taylor, at one point kicking her in the stomach and inducing a miscarriage. Taylor checked into Cedars of Lebanon Hospital for a week under a false name, while also dealing with the emotional turmoil that went with being beaten by her husband. (Kelley). Taylor finally had enough, as she later put it, "'He was drunk. I thought: 'This is not why I was put on Earth. God did not put me here to have a baby kicked out of my stomach.'" The marriage lasted just nine months, and the divorce was finalized on January 29, 1951, with Taylor citing verbal abuse as the reason for their divorce.

Taylor's first marriage was a fiasco, but it would be a mistake to simply describe it as a total catastrophe. Sexually inexperienced before meeting Hilton, it was with her first husband that she learned how to become more overtly sensual as she grew older. That newfound sensuality would appear quickly on screen. Taylor's first film after *Father of the Bride* was a sequel, *Father's Little Dividend* (1951), which was widely panned and simply an attempt to capitalize on the popularity of the earlier film, but her next film, *A Place in the Sun* (1951), was far more successful. Directed by acclaimed director George Stevens, the film paired Taylor with Montgomery Clift in the film adaptation of Theodor Dreiser's *An American Tragedy*. Clift occupies the starring role in the film as the working-class male who falls hopelessly in love with a wealthy girl. Already having impregnated his girlfriend, he considers killing her so that he can pursue a life with the wealthy girl. After taking his girlfriend on a boat ride, he does not save her when she falls off their boat and is eventually prosecuted for murder. Clift's character occupies the most prominent role, but Taylor excelled in her role as the object of his affection, and viewers could walk away arguing that she was never more glamorous. Biographer Kitty Kelley explains:

> "Elizabeth Taylor…personified the outer reaches of male fantasy. She was breathtakingly exquisite. Her velvet skin and black sable eyebrows framed eyes so deceptively blue they frequently looked violet. Her nose was perfectly chiseled and set above the sort of full and sensuous lips that produced the fantasies of adolescence in mature men and the soppiest of verse from serious poets…Spilling over with sex appeal, she was indeed the kind of girl American boys dreamed of marrying. Elizabeth Taylor was the ideal woman. She had the kind of beauty that would bring all a man ever dreamed of—wealth, fame, and position." (Kelley 37-38).

Taylor and Montgomery Clift in *A Place in the Sun*

   Elizabeth Taylor was ideally suited for the role of a wealthy girl who could drive a young man to contemplate murdering his girlfriend in order to pursue her. Still, working with George Stevens was a major challenge for her, as Stevens had a vastly different philosophy from Michael Curtiz, Vincente Minnelli, or any of the other directors with whom she had worked. Stevens endorsed method acting, the deeply psychological approach developed by Lee Strasberg at the Actor's Workshop in New York City. With his outward expressions of emotion, Montgomery Clift typified the method acting approach. On the other hand, Taylor did not have the training to perform in this manner, and there is a notable contrast between her and Clift onscreen that is potentially alienating for viewers. In a sense, the contrast between Clift and Taylor reflected the divide between method acting and the less-naturalistic style that had previously reigned supreme.

Despite the discrepancy between Clift and Taylor, *A Place in the Sun* was a major critical and commercial success. It was nominated for six Academy Awards, including Cinematography, Costume Design, Director, Editing, Score, and Screenplay. It was also nominated for Best Picture, Actor (for Montgomery Clift), and Actress (for Shelley Winters). The *New York Times'* critic, A.H. Weiler, argued, "Elizabeth's delineation of the rich and beauteous Angela is the top effort of her career", and a reviewer for *Boxoffice* asserted, "Miss Taylor deserves an Academy Award". Nevertheless, it is telling that Taylor was denied a nomination for her performance. At this stage of her career, she could occupy a supporting role in a critically acclaimed film, but she had not yet reached the point where she could win an Oscar.

Despite its success, *A Place in the Sun* did not immediately lead to a string of high-profile roles in critically successful films for Taylor. Her next significant appearance was a starring role in *Love is Better Than Ever* (1952), in which she starred as a dance instructor who romances a New York City talent agent. During the production, Taylor had an affair with director Stanley Donen, a relationship that drew the ire of MGM. Between 1951 and 1952, Taylor was also romantically linked to Howard Hughes, who was interested in marrying her, but Elizabeth's second husband would eventually be British actor Michael Wilding, who had divorced his wife a year earlier. Wilding was the polar opposite of Nicky Hilton or Howard Hughes, with a much gentler personality. Even though he was 20 years older than Elizabeth, the marriage received the full endorsement of MGM; according to Sam Kashner and Nancy Shoenberger, "It had been another marriage encouraged by MGM, to wipe out the bad publicity of her short-lived sting with Nicky, but Elizabeth had been attracted to Wilding, who seemed to offer stability and protection" (5). There may have been a significant age gap between them, but this marriage was more successful than her first, and Taylor gave birth to two sons, Michael (born 1953) and Christopher (born 1955) while married to him.

Taylor in 1954

Wilding in 1950

From 1952-1956, Taylor appeared in a series of unremarkable films, even while averaging two films per year. It was not until *Giant* (1956), which reunited her with George Stevens, that she again appeared in a major critical success. The film is most famous for being James Dean's last starring role before his fatal accident, but *Giant* also had several other prominent stars, including Taylor, Rock Hudson, and Mercedes McCambridge. Taylor stars as Leslie Lynnton, a socialite who marries Bick, a wealthy Texas rancher (played by Rock Hudson). As with all of his films, James Dean's over-the-top performance as the hired hand of Bick's sister distracts from the other characters, but the well-rounded film won the Academy Award for Best Director. It was also nominated for nine other awards, including Best Actor (for James Dean and Rock Hudson) and Best Actress (Mercedes McCambridge). Again, Taylor failed to receive a nomination, but *Giant* was a major milestone for her career and her first critically successful film in five years.

Taylor and Hudson in *Giant*

In a sense, *Giant* marked the birth of Elizabeth Taylor's career as a critically acclaimed actress, and the second half of the 1950s featured her in a number of similarly-praised films. In 1957, she starred in *Raintree County*, which once again paired her with Montgomery Clift and resulted in her first Academy Award nomination. Taylor and Clift starred together for a final time in *Suddenly, Last Summer* (1959), which earned Elizabeth another Academy Award nomination. Clift and Taylor remained close friends and may have had an affair together, but this seems unlikely in light of the fact that Clift was predominantly homosexual. When Clift suffered a notorious car accident that is widely viewed as the turning point in his life, he was leaving Taylor's home, and it was Taylor who ran to his aid.

Another film from this period that served a major role in furthering Taylor's career was the film adaptation of Tennessee Williams' *Cat On a Hot Tin Roof*, which was released in 1958 and also earned her another Academy Award nomination for Best Actress. Taylor starred as Maggie the Cat, the sexually deprived wife of an alcoholic, former high school track star. *Cat On a Hot Tin Roof* did not simply rely on the fame of Williams' play in order to garner its strong critical reception; it is on its own merits a significant film of late 1950s Hollywood. As described by Tanya Kryzwinska in *Sex and the Cinema*, *Cat On a Hot Tin Roof* was made during a period in which sex began to appear in a more explicit fashion, tailored specifically with an adult audience in mind. The legacy of the Hays Code, which had censored sexually suggestive material since its inception in the early 1930s, was in the process of losing its influence, and actresses such as Taylor, Marilyn Monroe, and (internationally) Brigitte Bardot began to portray sexuality much more overtly.

Taylor in *Cat On a Hot Tin Roof*

Ironically, it was not until 1960 that Taylor finally won her first Oscar, yet the film for which she won, *Butterfield 8*, is now largely forgotten. Building on the success of *Cat On a Hot Tin Roof*, Taylor once again starred as a sex-addicted heroine, appearing in *Butterfield 8* as an alcoholic prostitute. Taylor placed many demands on the shooting, including a stipulation that the film be shot in New York City rather than California, and she was ultimately not fond of the movie. Clearly, she had broken free from the innocent child star of the 1940s, transforming her star image into one more closely resembling that of a sex goddess and diva.

The final years of the 1950s also brought big change to Taylor's personal life, including two more marriages. Her short marriage to Wilding ended in a divorce that she blamed on herself, stating, "He was one of the nicest people I'd ever known. But I'm afraid I gave him rather a rough time, sort of henpecked him and probably wasn't mature enough for him." After divorcing Michael Wilding in 1957, she married Michael Todd just one week after the completion of the divorce. A major theater and film producer, Todd was well-known for having produced *Around the World in 80 Days*, which won the Academy Award for Best Picture in 1956, and for having co-developed the Todd-AO widescreen format, a film process that produced a widescreen image using just one camera. While married to Todd, she had her first daughter, Elizabeth (born 1957), but the marriage was brought to an abrupt end when Todd was killed in a plane crash on March 22, 1958. She was so distressed that she had to be physically restrained from jumping in his casket at the funeral, and one friend noted, "When she'd wake up, she'd just scream." Elizabeth's marriage to Todd was her only one that would not end in divorce.

Elizabeth Taylor with Mike Todd and their daughter, 1957

After Todd's death, Taylor did not wait long before marrying again. On May 12, 1959, she married Eddie Fisher, a close friend of Todd's, but that marriage came while Fisher was still married to Debbie Reynolds, creating a publicity scandal that only furthered Taylor's sultry reputation. The marriage to Fisher lasted nearly five years, but it was fraught with allegations of adultery. The same year that she married Fisher, Taylor also converted to Judaism, a change driven by her grief for Todd's death. She accepted the title Elisheba Rachel, and before converting, she studied Judaism for nine months (Taraborelli). She remained devoted to Judaism for the rest of her life.

The 1950s were an important decade for Elizabeth Taylor in many ways. The decade saw her become a critically acclaimed actress for the first time, all while she completely reshaped her image from the wholesome identity of a child star to a tempting vixen known for a string of marriages and affairs. Of course, there was a major parallel between the sex-starved roles she portrayed in her movies and the image of the restless wife she exuded off screen, and this similarity between her professional and personal life only heightened her popularity, making the public feel as though her films reflected the "real" Elizabeth Taylor. At the same time, though, people wondered why she would marry so many times if she could have simply had affairs without legally binding herself to another man. She would later state that she was old-fashioned, and that she only ended up sleeping with men she eventually married, but there would also appear to have been an emotional need for a male presence in her life that extended beyond the bedroom. At any rate, the many marriages and affairs reflect a tension in Taylor's identity. On the one hand, she welcomed the domestic status of the wife and raised several kids, yet at the same time she refused to sacrifice her career in the name of raising her family. Elizabeth's commitment to her career was almost feminist in nature, but she also embraced traditional roles by marrying and having children.

Chapter 7: The Marriage of the Century

"The unfortunate thing is that everyone wants me to play a prince or a king ... I'm always wearing a nightdress or a short skirt or something odd. I don't want to do them, I don't like them, I hate getting made up for them, I hate my hair being curled in the mornings, I hate tights, I hate boots, I hate everything. I'd like to be in a lounge suit, I'd like to be a sort of Welsh Rex Harrison and do nothing except lounge against a bar with a gin and tonic in my hand." - Richard Burton

"Eventually the inner you shapes the outer you, especially when you reach a certain age, and you have been given the same features as everybody else, God has arranged them in a certain way. But around 40 the inner you actually chisels your features. You know how some people have a kind of downward pull, and some people have sort of an upward pull, and look stress free, while the others look as if they're just trying to carry the world on their shoulders. You just want to say, shake your head, shake your body like a dog and just get rid of all that. It doesn't need to bow you down. Life is to be embraced and enveloped. Surgeons and knives have nothing to do with it. It has to do with a connection with nature, God, your inner being — whatever you want to call it — it's being in contact with yourself and allowing yourself, allowing God, to mold you." – Elizabeth Taylor

In 1961, Burton and Taylor finally crossed paths while working on yet another historical epic, the famous *Cleopatra*. The film was and remains one of the largest and most expensive in Hollywood history, costing $44 million in 1962 to make (the equivalent of roughly $310 million in 2014). When Taylor was offered $1 million by 20th Century Fox to star in *Cleopatra*, she jumped at the chance; she already yearned to leave MGM by 1960, but it was not until after completing *Butterfield 8* that she was given permission to prematurely end her contract. She had plenty of motivation, because, as she would later put it, "If someone's dumb enough to offer me a million dollars to make a picture, I'm certainly not dumb enough to turn it down." Her salary ultimately ballooned to $7 million, the modern day equivalent of $47 million.

Ironically, the movie's many troubles were what led to Burton being cast in one of his most pivotal roles. Stephen Boyd had originally been cast as Mark Antony, Caesar's right hand man and successor to Cleopatra's bed, but when Boyd had to drop out, Burton took his place. According to Burton, "Mark Antony is one of the great roles because it combines some of the best dialogue Shakespeare ever wrote and action; Antony was a man of action."

In many ways, the film is a celebration of Taylor's beauty, as she was featured in more than 60 different costumes and too many close-up shots to count. And even though production began in 1960, the film was not released until three years later. Rouben Mamoulian began as director but was eventually replaced by Joseph Mankiewicz. Furthermore, Taylor suffered from an eating disorder that kept her weight in constant fluctuation, so costumes had to be altered and scenes re-shot based on her ever-changing size. At one point, she fell so ill during production that a tracheotomy was performed in order to save her life. Burton and co-star Roddy McDowell would become so bored with the "hurry up and wait" nature of the production that they flew from Rome back to Hollywood to make cameo appearances in the World War II classic *The Longest Day* (1962).

Nonetheless, for Burton, Taylor was one of the most intriguing aspects of the movie. At times, he was dismissive of Taylor, once telling someone, "Well, I suppose I must don a breastplate once more to play opposite Miss Tits." On other occasions, he countered that the widely-held belief Taylor was "the most beautiful woman in the world is absolute nonsense. She has wonderful eyes, but she has a double chin and an overdeveloped chest, and she's rather short in the leg." However, when they met for the first time on stage, he approached her suavely and asked, "Has anyone ever told you that you're a very pretty girl?" She would later confess, "I said to myself, Oy gevalt, here's the great lover, the great wit, the great intellectual of Wales, and he comes out with a line like that." On top of that, Burton was in such awe of her that he had problems remembering his lines or hiding the fact that his hands shook when he took her in his arms. Charmed, she began to reach out to him during rehearsals, teaching him the many tricks of the trade she had learned through the years, and before long, Burton was more than comfortable being around her on screen and off screen. In fact, Sylvia, who had become accustomed to Burton's many dalliances, knew that this was something different and flew home to London with their daughters.

Burton and Taylor in *Cleopatra*

It's possible that the most memorable aspect of *Cleopatra* today is the romance that occurred off screen between Taylor and Burton, who almost seemed destined to engage in a high-profile affair. At the time, both were married, but they already had sexually promiscuous reputations. Moreover, during the early 1960s, Burton and Taylor were widely considered the two biggest sex icons in Hollywood, so their romance captured the public interest at an unprecedented level. For her part, Sylvia had no desire to go gently into the night and made sure that everyone on both sides of the Atlantic knew what was ending her marriage. Suddenly, everyone from the Vatican to Congress was issuing statements condemning the two famous adulterers and ordering them to return to their spouses. The scandal spread and rumors swirled around the production, leading Laurence Olivier to chide Burton in a telegram, "Make up your mind, dear heart. Do you want to be a great actor or a household word?" Burton cabled back, "Both." When he was called upon to publicly explain his adultery, Burton told one reporter, "The minute you start fiddling around outside the idea of monogamy, nothing satisfies anymore."

The one person who was happy about all the publicity was Zanuck, who was thrilled with the interest being stirred up in his movie. As a result of the quality of the production and the quantity of the hype, *Cleopatra* was a huge box-office hit, though it did not make as much money as it might have had it not cost so much to make. Although the film now appears as just another in a line of historical big-budget epics produced in the 1950s and early 1960s, it was well-received upon its release, winning Oscars for Best Art Direction, Cinematography, Costume Design, and Visual Effects. Professional critics were mixed with their reviews, with the *Time* review stating, "As drama and as cinema, Cleopatra is riddled with flaws. It lacks style both in image and in action." Critic Emanuel Levy said, "Much maligned for various reasons…Cleopatra may be the most expensive movie ever made, but certainly not the worst, just a verbose, muddled affair that is not even entertaining as a star vehicle for Taylor and Burton." On the other hand, *Variety* magazine noted, "Cleopatra is not only a supercolossal eye-filler (the unprecedented budget shows in the physical opulence throughout), but it is also a remarkably literate cinematic recreation of an historic epoch."

In addition to co-starring in *Cleopatra*, Taylor and Burton began an unofficial professional partnership, as they went on to start together in eight films during the 1960s. Following the completion of *Cleopatra*, Burton went on to make *The V.I.P.s* (1963), and he was cast opposite Taylor, thanks in large part to her insistence that she be given the role. Fortunately, the two of them were hot property in Hollywood at that time, and their off-screen lives attracted large audiences to the movie in spite of the film's poor reviews. The film grossed $15 million and was one of the most popular movies of that year. Burton at least pleased the critics, one of whom wrote, "Mr. Burton is better as the husband, particularly in the early scenes when he is weathering the shock of discovering the perfidy of his wife. Here he writhes in eloquent wrath and vengeance. It is when the defeat sinks in and he starts trying to crawl into the bottle that the frippipiness begins."

Burton's work in *Becket* (1964) earned him some of the best reviews of his career thus far. According to one critic, "Richard Burton makes [the character, Becket] a creature of contradictory nature and frigid, inflexible will. He is ready to compromise, to bargain in his early days with the king, but he assumes stoical rigidity when he takes on "the honor of God." There is little give in Mr. Burton's performance, little spirituality, little warmth. He is probably very close to the Becket of history."

By the time *The V.I.P.s* was released, Burton and Taylor were both well into the process of divorcing their respective spouses. No longer interested in putting up any kind of pretense, Taylor accompanied him to the on-location shooting for *The Night of the Iguana* (1964). Written by Tennessee Williams and directed by John Huston, the movie proved to be a huge hit, but some critics were not so crazy about Burton's performance, with one writing, "Mr. Burton is spectacularly gross, a figure of wild disarrangement, but without a shred of real sincerity. You see a pot-bellied scarecrow flapping erratically. And in his ridiculous early fumbling with the Lolitaish Sue Lyon (whose acting is painfully awkward), he is farcical when he isn't grotesque."

Burton and Ava Gardner in *The Night of the Iguana*

While working on *The Night of the Iguana*, Burton and Taylor travelled to Puerto Vallarta to film certain critical scenes. They ended up staying in a small fishing village for more than two months, long enough for Burton to fall in love with the island's quiet remoteness. He ended up buying a small house on the island as a private getaway.

Eventually, Taylor divorced Fisher and Burton divorced Sybil, after which the two of them got married on March 15, 1964 in Montreal, Canada. During the small ceremony, Taylor sported her engagement gift from Burton, an 18+ carat emerald and diamond brooch. Though it was Burton's second marriage and her fifth, Taylor was optimistic, telling one reporter, "I'm so happy you can't believe it. This marriage will last forever." He would later say of her, "Elizabeth has great worries about becoming a cripple because her feet sometimes have no feeling in them. She asked if I would stop loving her if she had to spend the rest of her life in a wheelchair. I told her that I didn't care if her legs, bum and bosoms fell off and her teeth turned yellow. And she went bald. I love that woman so much sometimes that I cannot believe my luck. She has given me so much." Of course, Burton gave Taylor a lot too, including a yacht, a 33 carat Krupp diamond, a 69 carat Cartier diamond and the historic Peregrina Pearl that was a gift from King Philip of Spain to his bride, Mary Tudor, in 1554.

Authors Sam Kashner and Nancy Schoenberger aptly summed up the enormous scale of the marriage: "Their thirteen-year saga was the most notorious, publicized, celebrated, and vilified love affair of its day. Indeed, their ten-year marriage, followed by a divorce, remarriage, and a final divorce, was often called 'the marriage of the century' in the press…So famous were the Burtons in the 1960s and 1970s that the duke and the duchess were their only peers, the only other couple who knew what it was like to be pariahs for a time, to pay a high price for their choices, and to live the rest of their lives in isolated luxury." That description reflects the unusual way in which marrying each other bore great consequences and risks for the two stars. On the one hand, they were tied to each other by marriage, but at the same time, Burton and Taylor were guaranteed to bask in public attention regardless of whether the marriage was successful. Still, there is no doubt that Richard Burton and Elizabeth Taylor were ideal spouses for each other, given how much both of them loved attention.

Burton and Taylor with Lucille Ball in 1974

Not long after their marriage, Burton adopted Taylor's daughter Liza, and the couple also adopted a little girl, Maria, who had been born in Germany in 1961. Content for a time, Burton turned his attention to writing by authoring the semi-autobiographical *A Christmas Story*. He was inspired in his writing by the famous *A Child's Christmas in Wales*, written by his celebrated friend, Dylan Thomas. Burton's effort was based on recollections from his boyhood and journals he had kept since he was 14 years old, though the book would not be published until several years later.

Chapter 8: Living, Loving and Working Together

"I am the son of a Welsh miner and one would expect me to be at my happiest playing peasants, people of the earth. But in actual fact I'm much happier playing princes and kings. Now whether this is a kind of sublimation of what I would like to be, or something like that, I don't know, but certainly I'm never really very comfortable playing people from the working class." - Richard Burton

"I might run from her for a thousand years and she is still my baby child. Our love is so furious that we burn each other out." - Richard Burton

Burton's professional and personal life were quite busy, but he always made time for stage work, and in 1964, he appeared in John Gielgud's production of *Hamlet*. From its opening in 1964, it went on to become the longest running Broadway play up until the time, running for a total of 136 performances. It remains famous and was the subject of both a soundtrack recording and a movie version created by filming and editing together several of the stage productions. Burton stumbled into this, one of his most famous roles, nearly by accident; while working on *Becket*, he made a deal with Peter O'Toole that each of them would later appear on stage as the lead in *Hamlet*, one in New York and one in London. Furthermore, one would be directed by John Gielgud while the other would be directed by Laurence Olivier. To decide who would get which location and which director, they flipped a coin, and Burton ended up with Gielgud in New York. Next, each man had to put together his production. Burton convinced Alexander Cohen to produce his version and convinced Gielgud to join them. O'Toole also successfully organized his version.

There were some problems, however. For one thing, Burton hated wearing Elizabethan clothing, so to keep him from having to don doublet and tights, Gielgud came up with the idea of putting on the play as if it were actually a rehearsal, like a play within a play. He even allowed his actors to choose their own clothing, though it did have to pass his strict standards. The play was a huge hit and ran for 137 performances, a record that still stands. Of course, Burton's relationship with Taylor boosted ticket sales, but critics also praised the play and Burton's performance, with one writing, "...for the first time, Hamlet is being played as Shakespeare wrote him -- he is indeed coldly objective, highly intelligent and virile." Burton was also nominated for a Tony Award for his role. The filmed version of the play was not as well received, running just two days.

Following his run in Hamlet, Burton starred in *The Spy Who Came in from the Cold* (1965), a role that earned him a David di Donatello Award for Best Foreign Actor and a Golden Laurel Award, as well as an Academy Award nomination for Best Actor in a Leading Role. It was also a significant box office hit and one of the top money makers of the year, but in the process, he missed out on the biggest spy role of that year. As he later recalled, "I almost replaced Sean Connery as James Bond in *Thunderball* (1965). This was before Sean played Bond. My friend, the Irish producer Kevin McClory, wanted me. Kevin worked for Michael Todd on *Around the World in Eighty Days* (1956) and I was impressed with his Irish rebelliousness. We Welsh have that, too, but not quite like the Irish, who transfuse it into their blood on the same day they are born. McClory promised [Alfred Hitchcock] would direct and I had great hopes for the project. It fell through, of course - and later Kevin made a bloody fortune, when Sean was Bond. I wonder sometimes how it might all have turned out. [Ian Fleming] was big on me for the role. Stewart Granger was next in line."

With the studio hoping to capitalize on the public's continued interest in Burton and Taylor, the two were cast as an adulterous couple in *The Sandpiper* (1965). Unfortunately, while the public flocked to the movie, critics were not so impressed, to the extent that one of them actually took insult: "Built up to give the impression that it is taking a disapproving view of an adulterous affair between a free-thinking woman and an Episcopal clergyman, it is really a slick and sympathetic sanction of the practice of free love—or, at least, of an illicit union that is supposedly justified by naturalness. And because it has Elizabeth Taylor and Richard Burton in the leading roles, the indelicacy of its implications is just that much more intrusive and cheap."

Burton and Taylor in *The Sandpiper*

Fortunately, not all of Burton and Taylor's efforts were such disappointments, even if they had to convince the powers that be to give them another chance. Thus, when Taylor was cast to star in *Whose Afraid of Virginia Woolf?* (1966), Burton worked to convince Warner executives to cast him opposite of her. Though the play's author, Edward Albee, was not crazy about the way the film was cast, director Mike Nichols proved that the two could still work together on screen.

The movie is set at a dinner party, where Burton and Taylor have friends over to their house for dinner. Over the course of the evening, the couple drinks heavily, which unearths their marital frictions in front of their embarrassed guests. Though audiences were initially shocked by the vulgar language and vicious remarks the two made to each other, the movie proved to be one of the most popular movies of that year and remains a classic today. According to one critic, "[Burton] has become a kind of specialist in sensitive self-disgust ... and he does it well. He is not in his person the George we might imagine, but he is utterly convincing as a man with a great lake of nausea in him, on which he sails with regret and compulsive amusement."

Of course, as with their other movies, the film was commercially successful not so much because of the script itself but because of the parallels it drew with the real life romance between Taylor and Burton. Since they were married in the film and in real life, the Burton-Taylor films contained a heightened degree of realism that transformed their films into must-see material. The film had such a lasting impact on both the Burton's and the public that later, when Taylor was trying to articulate the problems with her marriage, she exclaimed that she was "tired of playing Martha" to Burton's George. As Burton's younger brother also noted in an interview, "I think Richard became an alcoholic in the '60s. He always had to have a drink before he went onstage—he was very high-strung—but it never affected his performances. Then Elizabeth became an alcoholic. She certainly was not an alcoholic when I first knew her, although she used to like her Jack Daniel's. By the time they were making Who's Afraid of Virginia Woolf in 1966, they were both alcoholics. It must have been a Virginia Woolf situation in real life."

Burton and Taylor in *Who's Afraid of Virginia Woolf*

Regardless, the movie received a total of 13 Oscar nominations, including one each for Burton and Taylor. Taylor won her second Oscar for Best Actress, and for his role, Burton won a BAFTA Award for Best British Actor, a Bambi Award for Best International Actor and a Laurel Award for Top Male Dramatic Performance. He also took a second place in the National Society of Film Critics Award for Best Actor and the New York Film Critics Circle Award for Best Actor competitions.

Burton and Taylor in 1971.

By the mid-1960s, Burton had learned that life with Elizabeth Taylor was very different from that with any other woman. He soon found himself employing a team of support staff that included everyone from hairdressers to doctors, and lawyers to cooks. While the rest of the world might have been in awe of his glamorous wife, Burton certainly was not; in fact, he once shocked a reporter by saying, "At thirty-four she is an extremely beautiful woman, lavishly endowed by nature with a few flaws in the masterpiece: She has an insipid double chin, her legs are too short and she has a slight potbelly. She has a wonderful bosom, though." Of course, he was also well-known for this proclamation of devotion, "I love her, not for her breasts, her buttocks or her knees but for her mind. It is inscrutable. She is like a poem."

Continuing to work together, the two appeared together again in the disappointing *The Comedians* (1967). One critic summed up the problems with the movie this way: "The tired and disgusted hotel owner who would like to cut and run … is a character with many antecedents. And even though he is played with fine acerbity and bristling boredom by Richard Burton, he's a fellow we've all endured many times." Their last three films together, *Doctor Faustus* (1967), *The Comedians* (1967), and *Boom!* (1968), were all unsuccessful.

Nevertheless, Burton's movie career reached its American peak in 1966, when he was voted the 5th most popular actor in the United States. With his screen career taking more and more of his time, Burton made his final stage appearance for a decade in 1966, when he starred in *Doctor Faustus*. The following year, he produced and directed a film version of the play that would prove to be a critical and financial disappointment, and part of the problem appears to have been in the strong on-screen chemistry between him and Taylor, at least according to one critic: "The Burtons...are clearly having a lovely time; at moments one has the feeling that 'Faustus' was shot mainly as a home movie for them to enjoy at home. One or the other of them is almost constantly on camera—in various colors, flavors, and shades and lengths of hair...Burton, who has almost all the lines (the play has been quite badly cut) is worse. He seems happiest shouting in Latin, or into Miss Taylor's ear. The play's most famous lines sound like jokes in the context of so much celebrity: 'Was this the face that launched a thousand ships/ And burnt the topless towers of Ilium?' Well, no, one wants to say, but all the same . . ."

Burton and Taylor next starred together in *The Taming of the Shrew* (1967). For Burton, so long obsessed with the bard's plays, to make this film with the woman he loved must have been a dream come true. Their real life passion showed on film, and the movie was a box office success, but not everyone loved the film One critic complained, "I find it all grows a bit tedious. After we've examined Mr. Burton's great red beard, and Miss Taylor's … décolletage, listened to them toss about the language without much clarity or eloquence, watched Mr. Burton slobber drunkenly through scene after scene after scene, … it seems time to have done with clowning and settle down to a bit of comedy—comedy of a slightly adult order. The Burtons never do." Still, the movie earned Burton nominations for both a BAFTA and a Golden Globe.

Burton's next significant effort was producing and starring in *Where Eagles Dare* (1968), and his fingerprints are on every part of the movie, including the title, which was taken from Shakespeare's *Richard III:* "The world is grown so bad, that wrens make prey where eagles dare not perch." Burton also cast Clint Eastwood with him in the picture, and the movie remains notable for the harrowing fight scene that takes place atop a moving cable car.

Where Eagles Dare would not be the only movie Burton made in 1968, as he also starred in the embarrassing "sex farce" *Candy* (1968) opposite Marlon Brando. Burton's relationship with Brando was always complicated; on the one hand, he seemed to respect the man, saying in 1966, "He is a genuinely good man, I suspect, and he is intelligent. He has depth. It's no accident that he is such a compelling actor. He puts on acts, of course, and pretends to be vaguer than he is. Very little misses him, as I've noticed." However, a few years later, Burton called him "a smugly pompous little bastard and is cavalier about everybody except Black Panthers and Indians." What happened in the ensuing years is anyone's guess, but they did work on *Candy* together, so that might have had something to do with his change of attitude.

Burton suffered a very personal tragedy in 1968. He favorite brother, Ifor, was staying in his house when the two men stayed up late into the night drinking. While trying to make it back to his room, Ifor slipped and broke his neck, an accident that left him a quadriplegic and led to his early death in 1973. According to Burton's only younger sibling, Graham, the combination of these two events drove Burton deeper into the bottle than he had ever been before. Burton would later say, "I was up to, I'm told, because, of course, you don't remember if you drink that much, about two-and-a-half to three bottles of hard liquor a day. Fascinating idea, of course, drink on that scale. It's rather nice to have gone through it and to have survived." Burton was also smoking as many as 100 cigarettes a day. In the end, his addictions would cost him his marriage, his career, and ultimately his life.

Chapter 9: Making Rubbish

"If you're going to make rubbish, be the best rubbish in it. I keep telling Larry Olivier that. I chided Olivier for playing a minor role in an epic like Spartacus (1960), which he's just done. Larry had a dressing room half the size of Tony Curtis' in that film. And he got about half Curtis' money. Well, that's ridiculous. You've got to swank in Hollywood. When I go there I demand two Cadillacs - one for my family - and the best dressing room in the studio. Of course I'm not worth it, but it impresses them." - Richard Burton

By the late 1960s, it was obvious that Burton's best days in movies were behind him. One of his last big films was *Anne of a Thousand Days* (1969), in which he played Henry VIII to Genevieve Bujold's Anne Boleyn. Burton had no use for his co-star, saying about her, "I'd hate to be her next director or leading man. I think she firmly believes herself to be the legitimate heir to Rachelle or Bernhardt or Duse. She has all the power of a gnat. A dying one. I could whisper louder than her screams." Though the movie itself was a disappointment, Burton received some good reviews: "Burton…is in excellent form and voice—funny, loutish and sometimes wise…" He also earned nominations for an Oscar and a Golden Globe for his performance.

Burton's other significant role that year was opposite Rex Harrison in *Staircase* (1969), in which the two played the cutting edge roles of a homosexual couple. Discussing the controversy surrounding the movie, Burton maintained, "I believe in this film absolutely. It is a kick against the system." For Burton, it was just another role, for, as he observed, "I've played the lot: a homosexual, a sadistic gangster, kings, princes, a saint, the lot."

He made another kick against the system by insisting that the movie be shot in Paris so that he could avoid having to pay taxes in Great Britain, and Taylor also insisted that her latest movie, *The Only Game in Town* (1970), also be shot in Paris so that the two could be together. But in spite of its build up, the movie itself was both a box office and critical disappointment, even as the $1.25 million paycheck pushed Burton into the enviable position of being the highest paid actor in the world.

More honors lay just around the corner. When Burton was made a Commander of the British

Empire in 1970, he proudly showed off his success by inviting his beloved sister Cecilia to join him and Taylor at Buckingham Palace on the day of his investiture. The success did wonders on his outlook on life, and he was actually able to remain sober while making his next movie, *Raid on Rommel* (1970). On the other hand, he once admitted during an interview, "When I played drunks I had to remain sober because I didn't know how to play them when I was drunk."

Burton next starred in *Villain* (1971), and in a scene that was shocking at the time, Burton and co-star Ian McShane share an on-screen kiss. According to McShane, "He said to me, 'I'm very glad you're doing this film.' I said, 'So am I Richard.' He said, 'You know why, don't you?' I said, 'Why?' He said, 'You remind me of Elizabeth.' I guess that made the kissing easier." While Americans rejected the story of a bisexual man, the British embraced the tale, and it was a big hit in Britain. In fact, its success helped make him the most popular actor in Britain that year.

In spite of his celebrity back at home, Burton was quickly losing his grip on his American audience and on his own interest in acting. In 1972, he remarked, "I get increasingly disenchanted with acting ... as the years totter past I find it ludicrous, learning some idiot's lines in the small hours of the night so I can stay a millionaire." Of course, Burton was able to make a few movies he actually believed in, one of which was *Under Milk Wood* (1972), based on the last play written by Dylan Thomas. He again starred opposite Taylor, whom he enjoyed showing around his Welsh homeland during filming. Unfortunately, the rest of the film did not live up to the effort Burton put forth, leading to mixed reviews. One wrote, "When Burton urges us, the members of the audience, to look into 'the blinded bedrooms' to see 'the glasses of teeth, Thou Shalt Not on the wall, and the yellowing dickeybird-watching pictures of the dead,' there's not much for the camera to do but to try desperately to keep up with the language—but the language wins."

Burton returned to more classical material when he made *Bluebeard* (1972), but even though critics mostly despised it, a pictorial feature in *Playboy* boosted ticket sales and allowed the movie to see a small level of financial return. He next co-starred with Taylor in *Hammersmith is Out* (1972), which was filmed in Mexico and also bombed among critics and crowds. That movie is most memorable for Burton's role as a sociopath who never blinks.

1973 was an incredibly difficult year for Burton personally, because in addition to losing Ifor, he also had his marriage to Taylor break up. He seemed completely unable to find contentment anywhere, whether it be in front of a camera or on stage or in a bottle, and his discontentment bled over into his marriage, leading to a separation. The following year, in 1974, they divorced, but neither would ever completely get over the other, with Burton saying only months after their divorce was final, "I have a fair choice of women myself if I wish. But I don't wish it. Since Elizabeth, I have seen two. I've a fundamental and basic loyalty. Next year I'll be fifty and I've only been married twice. Yes, I betrayed them both a couple of times, but not mentally, only physically. You see, I may fall in love and it may last six months, but then the affair breaks up."

While it did not apparently rise to the level of an affair, Burton was quite mesmerized by his co-star in *The Voyage* (1974), Sophia Loren, saying, "She is as beautiful as an erotic dream. Tall and extremely large-bosomed. Tremendously long legs. They go up to her shoulders, practically. Beautiful brown eyes, set in a marvelously vulpine, almost satanic, face." Burton also starred opposite Loren again in the Hallmark Hall of Fame TV movie *Brief Encounter* (1974), but both of their projects together were critically panned.

Burton and Loren

During the 1970s, Taylor continued to maintain a tedious schedule, appearing in three films in both 1972 and 1973. Today, however, Taylor's films from 1970s onward are scarcely remembered, and though she divorced Burton again in 1976, she was married once again before the end of the year, this time to Virginia Senator John Warner in December. As Warner's wife, she lived in Washington, D.C., but she eventually grew depressed over her new lifestyle in the American capital. Taylor enjoyed interacting with the wives of the other senators, but she had not yet retired, and it became increasingly difficult for her to continue acting while married to Warner. They remained married until November 1982 but eventually separated. Unlike some of her earlier marriages, however, Elizabeth and Warner remained good friends even after the divorce was finalized.

John Warner

To a certain degree, Taylor's success as an actress correlated with the health of her marriage, and by the time of her divorce(s), she usually had only a fraction of her earlier box office appeal. Even so, she continued to remain productive. Her late-career highlights include the musical *A Little Night Music* (1977), in which she was cast in a somewhat autobiographical role as a famous actress who joins a group of friends and family for a weekend in the country. In 1980, she appeared in *The Mirror Crack'd* (1980), the large-budget film version of Agatha Christie's

The Mirror Crack'd from Side to Side. Playing the role of a famous actress making a career comeback after a long illness, the plot bore clear similarities with her own life, and she was a natural fit for the role. During the 1980s, her productivity waned and she began venturing into theater and television.

Taylor in 1981

Chapter 10: The Image as Epitaph

"Richard Burton is now my epitaph, my cross, my title, my image. I have achieved a kind of diabolical fame. It has nothing to do with my talents as an actor. That counts for little now. I am the diabolically famous Richard Burton." - Richard Burton

While some around him believed that he was actually more relaxed after his marriage ended, if anything, Burton was more medicated than happy. While working on *The Klansman* (1974) he was often too drunk to stand up during shooting, so he had to be filmed sitting down or sometimes even lying in bed. In some scenes, his voice was so slurred that his character appeared to have a speech impediment. Eventually, he drank so much in one sitting that he nearly died of alcohol poisoning, and after that experience he checked himself into the Saint

John's Health Center in Santa Monica to get help for his addiction. He explained his decision to seek help by mentioning, "The learned doctors told me if I continued to booze I should be prepared to welcome the end." He would later add, "I was fairly sloshed for five years. I was up there with John Barrymore and Robert Newton. The ghosts of them were looking over my shoulder." When asked why he was drinking so much at that time, Burton replied almost pitifully that it was "to burn up the flatness, the stale, empty, dull deadness that one feels when one goes offstage."

Of course, part of the reason that Burton was unable to give up drinking for any length of time was a simple absence of the desire for sobriety. He once summed up his attitude by saying, "I rather like my reputation, actually, that of a spoiled genius from the Welsh gutter, a drunk, a womanizer; it's rather an attractive image." Even when he and Taylor reconciled and re-married in 1975, he continued to drink, though claiming to be happy that they were back together.

In fact, it would remain for another woman, who was obviously not the great love of his life, to save him from himself, at least for a while from himself. In 1975, while making *Equus* (1977), Burton fell in love with Susan Hunt, and less than a year after marrying Taylor for a second time, the two again separated. Following their second divorce in 1976, Burton married Hunt. Herself a Hollywood outsider, she saw no need for the hard-partying life Burton was accustomed to and led him into a quieter, more sober existence. Though he did not give up drinking entirely, he cut way back and began to take better care of himself. For a change, he did not drink at all while making *The Wild Geese* (1978).

Playing against type, Burton starred as a priest in *The Exorcist II: The Heretic* (1977). After some success in the role, he went on to play a priest again in *Absolution* (1978). It proved to be one of his last great roles, with the director observing, "You can see Richard Burton in these landscapes, can't you? He's marvelous in the part of Goddard. He has that huge, outsize quality, rather like Russian actors. There's nothing too small or mean about Richard's acting. At the moment he is just getting into the part because he has only been filming for a week…Also Goddard has a sadistic streak, which Richard is bringing out in the character with such subtly. He has that marvelous dry, cutting edge which he used so brilliantly in Virginia Woolf."

Burton returned to the stage in 1980 during a Broadway revival of *Camelot*, but he had injured his back and was in constant pain, which he treated with increasing doses of prescription painkillers to the point that he was no longer able to act. He was replaced just a few months into the play's tour, and he then checked himself into a hospital and had surgery to fuse the vertebrae in his neck. He would remain stiff in his movements for the rest of his life, telling one reporter "I don't have tremendous physical vitality since I had a neck operation, and I'm more aware than I used to be of the tedium of acting." By this time, the alcohol had also taken a toll on his physical abilities, as his younger brother recounted, "Richard's breakfast was a large glass of vodka with some tomato juice, Worcestershire sauce and lemon, always referred to as 'my three-course breakfast.' In London in 1981, a doctor showed me an X ray of Richard's liver, and it was three times the size of a normal liver. Early one morning in the Dorchester hotel, I found him pouring vodka. I said in Welsh, 'You're killing yourself.' He answered in Welsh, 'So be it.' He said he felt that he'd already done everything in his professional work and there was so little left to do. But he was angry and drunk and as usual saying things he didn't mean."

In 1982, Burton starred opposite his daughter Kate in a Broadway version of *Alice in Wonderland*, and the play was such a hit that PBS videotaped one of the performances and showed it on television. That same year, Burton met Sally Hay, a production assistant working on the set of his latest film, *Wagner* (1982), in which he played the title role. Unlike his previous wives, Hay was a liberated, independent woman used to taking care of herself, and Burton soon learned that she was also willing to take care of him, telling one friend, "She can do everything…there's nothing she can't do…she looks after me so well. Thank God I've found her." He soon divorced Hunt and began to make plans for a permanent future with Hay, and he was also hoping that he might revive his career, saying in a 1982 interview, "You reach the top of the heap, but it's a circle, and you slip on the down side; maybe for years. You get scared."

In the meanwhile, he found himself once more starring opposite Taylor, this time in a stage version of Noel Coward's *Private Lives* in 1983. After one poor rehearsal, he noted, "ET impossibly sloshed all day long. So much so she couldn't even read the lines." However, though they were now with different spouses, Burton continued to remain fixated on his ex-wife, at least according to his younger brother: "I saw Richard at the Dorchester about six weeks before he died. He kept talking about Elizabeth as if she were there. Or he'd say, 'I was speaking to Elizabeth on the phone today. Never a day goes by. She's a remarkable woman. I must tell you she's forgotten more about screen acting than I'll ever learn, but I think I can show her a thing or two onstage.' The next thing, he'd say, 'Elizabeth, fill Graham's glass,' and I'd whisper to him, 'That's Sally.' And he'd swear to himself in Welsh. He said, 'I'm always doing that.'"

With his life looking up, he married Hay in Los Vegas and began to make plans to return to London to appear once more at the Old Vic. After *Private Lives* completed its run, he and Hay travelled to Haiti for a very long honeymoon before returning to Celigny, and when they finally got back to France, Burton began work on *Nineteen Eighty-Four* (1984), which would prove to be his last movie. Later that year, he appeared on television a final time in the mini-series *Ellis Island*. He and Hay then returned to their home in Geneva, Switzerland, for a rest before he began work on *Wild Geese II*.

On August 5, 1984, Burton began complaining of a severe headache, and just a few hours later, he was dead of a cerebral hemorrhage. Hay had his body returned to Celigny for burial, where he was laid to rest holding a copy of *The Collected Poems of Dylan Thomas* and dressed in a red suit, in keeping with his Welsh heritage. When asked about his old friend, Sir John Gilegud said, "He was serious, charming, with tremendous skill. I feel nothing but sadness. He chose a rather mad way of throwing away his theater career but obviously he became very famous and a world figure through being a film star. He was awfully good to people and generous." Sir Lawrence Olivier added, "Richard was a very fine actor and his early death is a great tragedy to the theater world, the film world and the public."

The one person who did not speak out publically at that time was Elizabeth Taylor. Rumors still abounded about the couple, with some saying that they had made plans to be buried side by side. Whether or not that was true, Hay made sure that it would never happen by purchasing the burial plot next to Burton and placing a large headstone across both places, setting aside room for only herself in her husband's afterlife. Hay also ensured Burton's diaries and notes were published in the 21st century, which offered both explosive commentary about his contemporaries and inner reflections about his own life. Though people were more interested in what Burton had to say about people like Taylor, Hay had a different take on the tenor of Burton's writings: "Having been rescued from the Co-op, I think his attitude was, how far can I take this? It was his personal adventure – look how far from Wales this boy has gone."

Chapter 11: Taylor's Later Years

Taylor at the American Film Festival of Deauville in France, 1985

"For me, life happened, just as it does for anyone else. I have been supremely lucky in my life in that I have known great love, and of course … some incredible and beautiful things." –

Elizabeth Taylor

By the mid-1980s, it was clear that Elizabeth Taylor could no longer command major box office success, which did not reflect any deficiency in her acting but merely the tendencies of growing old in Hollywood. Even still, she remained extremely popular, and one of the most unusual aspects of her stardom is that her personal life attracted more attention than her actual films. During the 1980s, she was in the news on several occasions for all sorts of different reasons. In 1983, she checked herself into the Betty Ford Center for an addiction to prescription drugs, and she relapsed later in the decade. In 1990, an attorney general investigation found that Taylor had received prescriptions for more than two dozen prescription drugs, and she admitted to abusing prescription drugs for decades (Heymann). Later in the decade, Taylor became an outspoken advocate on behalf of AIDS sufferers, raising over $270 million for the cause. She co-founded the American Foundation for AIDS Research and was awarded a special Academy Award for her efforts in 1992. As she put it, "Acting is, to me now, artificial. Seeing people suffer is real. It couldn't be more real. Some people don't like to look at it in the face because it's painful. But if nobody does, then nothing gets done."

Her weight also attracted public attention because it changed wildly. In 1987, she published a dieting book, *Elizabeth Taylor Takes Off*, but she was unable to maintain a consistent weight herself. The constant fluctuations in her appearance made her fodder for tabloid magazines, but according to the old adage, there's no such thing as bad publicity. Taylor also maintained high-profile friendships late in life, counting Michael Jackson among her more famous friends. After his death in 2009, she said, "My heart…my mind… are broken. I loved Michael with all my soul and I can't imagine life without him. We had so much in common and we had such loving fun together."

In 1991, Taylor married Larry Fortensky, a construction worker she met during a rehabilitation stay at the Betty Ford Center. The marriage ceremony was held at Jackson's Neverland Ranch, but as with Taylor's earlier marriages, it ended in divorce. The divorce was finalized on October 31, 1996, and Fortensky would be Elizabeth's final husband. In many ways, the number of marriages and husbands is one of the best known parts of Taylor's life, and even as far back as 1965, she felt she had been married too many times, noting, "I've been married too many times. How terrible to change children's affiliations, their affections — to give them the insecurity of placing their trust in someone when maybe that someone won't be there next year."

During the 1990s, Taylor continued to appear on television, guest-starring in episodes of *The Simpsons* and other shows, and even into the 21st century, she continued to attend prominent entertainment events and remained a popular figure. In a surprising development, although hardly abnormal among Hollywood stars, she deviated from her earlier Republican beliefs and became an outspoken critic against President George W. Bush and the Iraq War. In 2007, she appeared on-stage for the final time, in an AIDS fundraiser, but by this time, she had already begun suffering from heart disease. Taylor survived a number of ailments, which included hip replacements, skin cancer, and even a brain tumor, but she eventually died of congestive heart failure at the age of 79 on March 23, 2011.

Though she is remembered mostly for her life and career as an adult, Elizabeth Taylor still stands out as one of the few child stars who were successfully able to retain their popularity as an adult. Her performances in *Lassie Come Home* and *National Velvet* solidified her status as one of the most famous child actresses of all time, but her performances during the 1950s (especially *A Place in the Sun*, *Giant*, and *Cat On a Hot Tin Roof*) were every bit as popular and catapulted her to superstardom. She did not reach her peak until her most famous films with Richard Burton the following decade. Taylor's films are not often listed as among the best ever made, but she still won two Academy Awards, and she was able to overcome the pressures of being a star for nearly 70 years.

The longevity of Taylor's career is remarkable, but it is also important to note that the Elizabeth Taylor who first captivated America during World War II was hardly the same person who won Academy Awards or became an AIDS activist. After all, her life contained several chapters, from child actress to sultry sex icon to wife of Richard Burton to activist. As such, the genius of Elizabeth Taylor was not only that she was able to remain in the public spotlight for so long but that she managed to successfully reinvent her image as she grew older. As such, her life has been subjected to wildly different interpretations. On the one hand, she was for many years considered a conservative icon, but M.G. Lord is also correct when she notes that Taylor was in some respects a feminist. Her universal appeal derived from the fact that she appealed to people for different reasons, all while managing to avoid alienating any specific group.

Throughout the many phases of her life and career, the one common factor is that Elizabeth Taylor thrived in the spotlight. As she transitioned from child to adult, her image was no longer clean-cut, and throughout her life it is easy to spot the joys and sorrows of being a Hollywood star. To this end, Camille Paglia argues, "Elizabeth Taylor is a creation of show business, within which she has lived since she began as a child star…Elizabeth Taylor, heartily eating, drinking, lusting, laughing, cursing, changing husbands, and buying diamonds by the barrel, is a personality on a grand scale. She is a monarch in an age of glub liberals" (18). Taylor was among the most glamorous figures in Hollywood, yet she was still accessible enough for the public to relate to her. For many, the pressure of living in the entertainment industry lead to resentment, but Taylor recognized her privileged life and appeared to genuinely enjoy the lifestyle.

Bibliography

Bragg, Melvyn. *Rich. The Life of Richard Burton.* Little Brown & Co.; 1st U.S. edition (1989).

Bret, David. *Elizabeth Taylor: The Lady, the Lover, the Legend.* Vancouver: Greystone Books,

2011. Print.

Brodie, Fawn M. *The Devil Drives: A Life of Sir Richard Burton.* W. W. Norton & Company; Reprint edition (1984)

Burton, Richard. *The Richard Burton Diaries.* Yale University Press; 1st edition (2012).

Heymann, C. David. *Liz: An Intimate Biography of Elizabeth Taylor*. New York: Atria, 2011. Print.

Kashner, Sam, and Nancy Schoenberger. *Furious Love: Elizabeth Taylor, Richard Burton, and the Marriage of the Century*. New York: HarperCollins, 2010. Print.

Kelley, Kitty. *Elizabeth Taylor: The Last Star*. New York: Simon & Schuster, 1981. Print.

Kryzwinska, T. *Sex and the Cinema*. London: Wallflower Press, 2006. Print.

Lord, M.G. *The Accidental Feminist: How Elizabeth Taylor Raised Our Consciousness (And We Were Too Distracted By Her Beauty to Notice.)* New York: Walker & Company, 2012. Print.

Munn, Michael. *Richard Burton: Prince of Players.* Skyhorse Publishing. (2008)

Paglia, Camille. *Sex, Art, and American Culture: Essays*. Toronto: Random House, 1992. Print.

Papa, Joseph. *Elizabeth Taylor, A Passion for Life: The Wit and Wisdom of a Legend*. New York: HarperCollins, 2011. Print.

Rubython, Tom. *And God Created Burton.* Myrtle; 1St Edition. (2011)

Taraborelli, J. Randy. *Elizabeth*. New York: Warner, 2006. Print.

Taylor, Elizabeth. *Elizabeth Taylor's Nibbles and Me*. New York: Simon & Schuster, 2002. Print.

Walker, Alexander. *Elizabeth: The Life of Elizabeth Taylor*. New York: Conundrum Limited, 1997. Print.

Wright, Thomas. *The Life of Sir Richard Burton.* Amazon Digital Services, Inc. (2011)

Printed in Great Britain
by Amazon.co.uk, Ltd.,
Marston Gate.